Mrs Wordsmith®

YEAR 6 ENGLISH

MONUMENTAL WORKBOOK

MEET THE
CHARACTERS

Yang

Bogart

Oz

Yin

Armie

Brick

Shang High

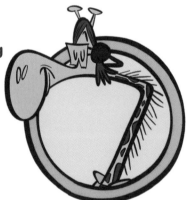

Bearnice

Grit

Plato

This book belongs to:

....

CONTENTS

Welcome to the Year 6 Monumental Workbook!

What's inside?

In this book, you will find everything you need to breeze through English in Year 6. It is divided into five chapters: **Grammar**, **Punctuation**, **Vocabulary**, **Spelling** and **Reading and Writing**. Each chapter combines targeted teaching of key skills, illustrations and activities. It's perfect for those learning something for the first time and for those who are just revising!

How do I use it?

However you want to! Start in the middle, start at the end or you could even start at the beginning if you're feeling traditional. Take it slowly and do one section at a time, or charge through the pages like a raccoon on the loose! Don't worry if something is too difficult. You'll get there in the end and there are tips and reminders to help you along the way.

Look out for this icon at the beginning of a new topic. It tells you that there's some important learning to do before you start answering the questions!

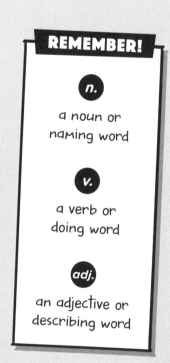

REMEMBER!

n.
a noun or naming word

v.
a verb or doing word

adj.
an adjective or describing word

How do I check my answers?

There's an answer key at the back! Checking answers is an important part of learning. Take care to notice and remember the ones you didn't know.

Oh, and please excuse Mrs Wordsmith's cast of out-of-control animals. They pop up all over the place and are usually up to no good.

Now, go and have some fun! And who knows, you might learn something along the way.

GRAMMAR

Grammar teaches you how to use different kinds of words (like verbs, nouns or adjectives) in all of their forms and to construct different kinds of sentences. When you master basic grammar rules, you have the power to talk or write about anything. When you master some more advanced grammar rules, you have the power to write beautifully.

Remember, a noun is the name of a person or animal, place or thing.

Proper nouns name specific people or animals, places or things.
These always begin with a capital letter.

Bearnice　　Monday　　August

Common nouns name general places or things.

chicken
table
happiness

Collective nouns name groups of people, animals or things.

swarm of flies
litter of puppies
fleet of ships

All nouns are either **concrete** or **abstract**.

Concrete nouns are physical things that you can see and touch.

chicken　table
swarm

Abstract nouns are things without a physical form, like a concept or idea.

Monday　August
happiness

1 Circle the proper nouns and underline the common nouns.

a. Grit wrote a poem.

b. Oz's sculpture started to melt.

c. Brick had always wanted to visit Thailand.

d. Armie has lessons on Tuesdays.

e. "Whose restaurant is this?" asked Plato.

f. The factory exploded.

2 **Circle the abstract nouns and underline the concrete nouns in these sentences.**

a. He thanked his teacher for her generosity.

b. She was wearing her trousers backwards again.

c. He demanded freedom after she locked him in the shed.

d. The firefighter saved the cats and returned them to their houses.

e. Her bedroom was utter chaos.

3 **Draw lines to match the noun to its noun type.**

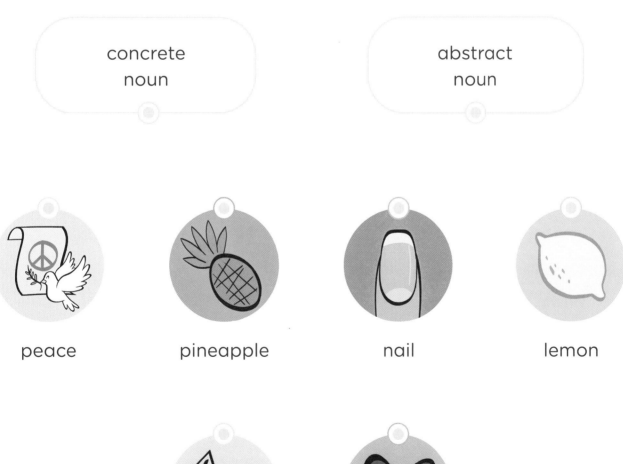

concrete noun

abstract noun

peace

pineapple

nail

lemon

danger

love

Verbs are **doing** and **being** words. A **doing** word describes an action (for example, **run** is a doing word). A **being** word describes a state of being (for example, **am** is a being word).

But what happens when nouns and verbs collide? Some words can take the form of a noun or a verb. Look out for context clues to help you identify if a word is used as a noun or a verb in the sentence.

To check if a word is used as a noun in a sentence, try saying **the**, **an**, **a** or a possessive adjective (**my**, **your**, **his**, **her**) before it. If the sentence still makes sense, it's a noun. For example,

You have an evil **laugh**.

To check if a word is used as a verb in a sentence, try saying **I** or **you** before it. If the sentence still makes sense, it's a **verb**. For example,

You **laugh** in an evil way.

Word	Example sentence
challenge	**Noun:** Grit sometimes found socialising to be a **challenge**. **Verb:** Yang decided to **challenge** Yin to a duel.
smell	**Noun:** "What's that **smell**?" grumbled Grit. **Verb:** Grit used his sensitive nose to **smell** a single pea under his mattress.

1 Read through these sentences.

The underlined words are either a noun or a verb.
Write **N** for noun and **V** for verb in the gaps next to the sentences.

a. Bogart had to <u>face</u> the consequences of his actions. ◯

b. "Pass me the <u>whistle</u>," grumbled Brick. ◯

c. Grit scowled as Oz blew him a <u>kiss</u>. ◯

d. Bearnice can <u>name</u> all the planets in the solar system. ◯

e. They hid behind the sofa, waiting to <u>surprise</u> Bogart. ◯

f. Bogart was forced to pay for all the <u>damage</u> he caused. ◯

g. "What is your <u>name</u>?" asked Armie. ◯

2 Now it's your turn!

Write your own sentence using the word **promise**
as a noun in one sentence and as a verb in another.

a. Noun:

....

....

....

b. Verb:

....

....

....

Most simple sentences have a **subject**, a **verb** and an **object**.

The **subject**, which usually comes first,
is often the person or thing doing the verb.

The **verb**, which usually comes after the subject,
is a doing or being word.

The **object**, which usually comes after the verb,
often has something done to it by the verb.

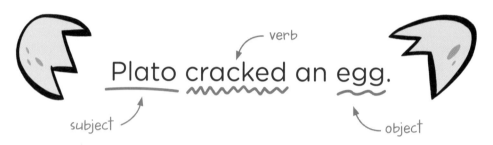

verb

Plato cracked an egg.

subject

object

TIP!

Sometimes, the subject of the sentence is not doing anything. Instead, it is having
something done to it. This is called the passive voice and is covered on page 22.

1 **Underline the subject and circle the object of each sentence.**

a. Bogart mocked Brick.

b. Grit wagged his tail.

c. Bearnice watched a film.

d. The ghost haunted the mansion.

e. Armie opened the vault.

f. Shang High bought a guitar.

2 Label the underlined words as either S (subject), O (object) or V (verb).

a. Oz <u>borrowed</u> Armie's artificially intelligent robot.

b. <u>Bogart</u> shouted at the television.

c. Plato <u>chased</u> the taco truck.

d. Yin tickled <u>Yang</u>.

e. Brick dropped his <u>sunglasses</u>.

f. Shang High <u>waved</u> at Grit.

3 Complete the sentence by adding a subject or object.

a. **Subject:** .... played the kazoo.

b. **Object:** Bogart likes eating ....

c. **Subject:** .... won an

eight-metre-tall jar of jelly beans.

d. **Object:** Plato stirred ....

e. **Object:** Bearnice smashed ....

f. **Object:** Oz knitted ....

Tense tells us when something takes place.
Things can happen in the **past**, **present** or **future**.
When a sentence has more than one verb in it,
they are usually in the same tense.

The past is used to describe actions
that have already happened.

Oz **slept** peacefully last night.

The present tense is used to describe actions that
are happening now or happen regularly.

Oz **sleeps** peacefully.

REMEMBER!

When the subject is singular, add –s to the present tense verb.
When the subject is plural or the subject is I or you,
do not add –s to the present tense verb.

The future tense is used to describe actions
that will happen in the future.

Oz **will sleep**
peacefully tonight.

Verb tense	Past	Present	Future
Simple	I played tennis.	I play tennis.	I will play tennis.
Progressive	I was playing tennis.	I am playing tennis.	I will be playing tennis.
Perfect	I had played tennis.	I have played tennis.	I will have played tennis.

The **present tense** is used to talk about things that are constantly true and do not change, like habits, emotions and repeated actions.

Oz **likes** her own reflection.
Armie **reads** every day.

The **past tense** is used to talk about actions that have finished.

Plato **cooked** for everyone.
Bogart **crashed** into a tree.

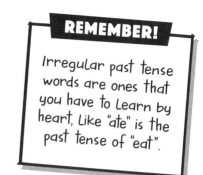

REMEMBER!

Irregular past tense words are ones that you have to learn by heart, like "ate" is the past tense of "eat".

1 Draw lines to match the sentence to the correct tense.

present tense

past tense

Grit watches
TV every day.

Bearnice accidentally tied
her shoelaces together.

Oz slept through
the whole movie.

Armie wakes
up at 6am.

2 Rewrite these present tense sentences in the past tense.

a. Yang loves spinach.

....

b. Bearnice always forgets her pencils.

....

When we want to write about something that is still happening, we use the **present progressive** tense. This is made with the present tense form of **to be** (**is**, **am** or **are**) plus the **main verb** with -**ing** at the end.

is, am or are + verb + -ing
Bearnice is laughing.

The **past progressive** is made in the same way but with the past tense form of **to be** (**was** or **were**). It is used to talk about an action that was happening for a period of time in the past.

was or were + verb + -ing
Bearnice was laughing.

1 **Complete these sentences in the present progressive tense by adding is, am or are.**

a. Bearnice and Brick .... acting in a play.

b. Oz .... wearing a flower crown.

c. You .... disagreeing.

d. I .... confessing to a crime.

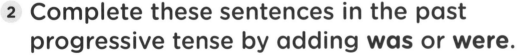

2 **Complete these sentences in the past progressive tense by adding was or were.**

a. Grit .... gardening.

b. The horses .... galloping.

c. You .... brewing a potion.

d. She .... snoring loudly.

3 Draw lines to match the sentence to the correct tense.

Bogart was sending anonymous hate mail.

Oz is singing in front of the mirror.

Yang is firing arrows from behind the trees.

present progressive

Shang High was wearing a helmet.

past progressive

Bearnice is hiding the note inside a locket.

Armie was hacking into the company's database.

Plato is drinking maple syrup straight from the bottle.

4 Write a sentence about what you **were** doing before you opened your workbook.

I was ....

....

The **present perfect tense** is used to talk about something that happened in the past at an unspecified time. It is formed using the present tense form of **to have** followed by the main verb in the past tense.

'to have' verb in the present tense

Plato has cooked a lasagne.

Main verb in the past tense

The **past perfect** form of a verb is used to refer to an action that finished before another action in the past. It is formed using the past tense form of **to have** followed by the main verb in the past tense.

'to have' verb in the past tense

Plato had cooked a lasagne before his dinner guests arrived.

Main verb in the past tense

1 Past simple or present perfect?

Read the sentences and write whether it is **past simple (PS)** or **present perfect (PP)**.

TIP!

Here are some examples to help you.
Present perfect: I have played tennis. Past simple: I played tennis.

a. Shang High has broken the world record. ◯

b. Bogart has changed everyone's passwords. ◯

c. Armie invented a new type of four-dimensional graph. ◯

d. Bearnice and Armie have heard two crashes of thunder. ◯

e. Yin and Yang inspired each other to cause trouble. ◯

2 Complete these sentences in the **past perfect** form.

Use the past tense form of the verb **to have** and the past tense form of the verb in brackets. The first one is done for you.

a. When I arrived at the cinema, the film _____had started_____. **(start)**

b. Oz _____ the contestants before the talent show

had even begun. **(judge)**

c. Plato _____ the wildlife before it got dark. **(photograph)**

d. Before she left, Bearnice _____ off all the lights. **(turn)**

e. Grit _____ in traffic for three hours before he started

to scream. **(wait)**

3 Write two **present perfect** sentences about the images below.

Use the three keywords listed to get you started. For example, if the key words were **cake**, **eat** and **Yin**, your sentence might be **Yin has eaten the whole cake**.

a. **destroy**   **Bearnice**   **cake**

_____

_____

b. **Armie**   **buy**   **car**

_____

_____

Sentences can be formed in the active or the passive voice.
In the active voice, the subject of the sentence is doing the action
of the verb. We use the active voice more commonly because it makes
the meaning of a sentence simpler and clearer.

In the passive voice, the subject of the sentence is not doing anything.
Instead, it is having something done to it. We use the passive voice
to focus on the person or object experiencing the action
(rather than the person or object performing the action).

The subject is doing the action.

active voice:

Armie read the book.

The subject is having the action done to it.

passive voice:

The book was read by Armie.

The subject is doing the action.

Shang High juggled three balls.

The subject is having the action done to it.

Three balls were juggled by Shang High.

① Rewrite the following in the passive voice.

a. Yang destroyed the table.

....

....

....

b. Plato ate all the burgers.

....

....

....

c. Oz drove the brand new sports car.

....

....

....

d. Armie rode the red bike.

....

....

....

2 Are these sentences written in the passive or active voice?

The passive voice does not always tell you who or what did the action.
You can say **The plants were watered by Grit** or you can just say
The plants were watered. Both of these sentences are passive.

TIP!

Sometimes this form is used deliberately when you don't know who did the action.
For example, a police report might read "the jewels were stolen" because the police
don't yet know who stole them.

Write **P** (for **passive**) or **A** (for **active**) above each sentence. If you get stuck,
ask yourself whether the subject of the sentence is doing the action.

a.

Oz watered
the cactus.

b.

The trees
were cut down
by Bogart.

c.

Shang
High wrote
a new song.

d.

All the
tacos were
eaten.

Modal verbs are used to change the meaning of other verbs.

The main modal verbs are **will**, **would**, **can**, **could**, **may**, **might**, **shall**, **should**, **ought** and **must**. These can express degrees of possibility as well as permission or obligation.

Brick **might** go to Bogart's party.

Might is the modal verb here, used to express the likelihood of Brick going to the party. It means that it is not certain that Brick will go, but there is a chance that he will.

Modal verb	How it's used	What it means
will (past tense: would)	She **will** sing later today.	It is certain that she will sing in the future (possibility).
can (past tense: could)	She asks if she **can** sing.	She is asking to sing (permission).
may (more formal than might)	She **may** sing later.	There is a chance she will sing in the future (possibility).
might (less formal than may)	She **might** sing later.	There is a chance she will sing in the future (possibility).
shall	She **shall** sing beautifully.	She intends to sing beautifully in the future (possibility).
should	She **should** sing now.	It is necessary for her to sing (obligation).
ought	She **ought** to sing now.	It is very necessary for her to sing (obligation).
must	She **must** sing now.	It is extremely necessary for her to sing (obligation).

1 Read the sentences and answer the questions.

a. **Armie asks if he can go to sleep.**

   Oz must go to sleep.

   Who requests permission to go to sleep?

   ....

b. **Brick may fall over.**

   Shang High will fall over.

   Who is more likely to fall over?

   ....

c. **Plato must make soup.**

   Grit should make soup.

   For whom is it more necessary to make soup?

   ....

2 Now it's your turn!

Write a sentence for each prompt, using and underlining a modal verb in each to show how likely the event is to happen. The first one is done for you.

a. Travel the world: *I will travel the world when I'm older.*

b. Learn a new sport: ....

c. Move to a new country: ....

d. Learn how to drive: ....

e. Become a famous singer: ....

....

As you may already know, **a**, **an** and **the** are **articles**.
They appear before nouns or noun phrases.

A comes before **nonspecific** nouns or noun phrases beginning
with **consonant sounds**, like **a trumpet** or **a golden trumpet**.

An comes before **nonspecific** nouns or noun phrases beginning
with **vowel sounds**, like **an orangutan** or **an energetic orangutan**.

The is used when talking about **specific** nouns or noun phrases,
like **the trumpet** or **the orangutan**.

Articles are a type of **determiner**. **Determiner** is a term that covers
a range of words. These words specify or provide information about
a noun or noun phrase. As well as articles, these can include the following.

Demonstratives show where an object,
event or person is in relation to the speaker.

Singular nouns: **this** (nearby),
that (far away)

Plural nouns: **these** (nearby),
those (far away)

This shoe is nearby.
That shoe is far away.

These hats are nearby.
Those hats are far away.

Possessives show belonging and include the possessive pronouns
mine, yours, his, hers, its and theirs.

His shoes are green.   **Her** laces are blue.

Quantifiers often show how much or how many.

She lost **some** socks in the wash.
Bearnice invited a **few** friends over.

TIP!

When trying to identify determiners, it can be helpful
to first identify the noun or noun phrase.

---

1 Circle the determiners in these sentences.

a. Yin loves this waterpark.

b. Plato ate his waffles in a few seconds.

c. Bearnice eats apples every day.

d. Bogart plans to use these tools to take over the city.

e. Shang High lost those gloves last night.

f. Oz has many hobbies.

2 Circle the correct determiner.

a. To make   **this**   **those**   lasagne, you will need   **a**   **an**   onion.

b.   **Our**   **These**   house was built in the 1800s.

c.   **Those**   **That**   earrings are beautiful!

d. "I love   **few**   **your**   friends!" exclaimed Oz.

e.   **A**   **Many**   people can tightrope walk.

f. "What are you doing with   **these**   **my**   book!" cried Armie.

g. Bearnice picked   **those**   **more**   apples than Oz.

Pronouns are short words that can take the place of nouns in a sentence. Without pronouns, sentences can get repetitive very quickly.

Subject pronouns replace the noun that acts as the subject (the noun performing the action) in the sentence.

Singular subject pronouns: **I you he she it they**
Plural subject pronouns: **we you they**

Oz gazed at the mirror in awe.　　**She** gazed at the mirror in awe.

Object pronouns replace nouns that act as the object (the noun that the action is done to) in the sentence.

Singular object pronouns: **me you him her it them**
Plural object pronouns: **us you them**

Bearnice followed **Armie** home.　　Bearnice followed **him** home.

Possessive pronouns replace nouns that show who owns something.

Singular possessive pronouns: **mine yours his hers its theirs**
Plural possessive pronouns: **ours yours theirs**

The cunning plan is **Bogart's**.　　The cunning plan is **his**.

The noun has an apostrophe to show possession.

TIP!

The pronouns they, them and theirs can refer to more than one person, a person whose gender you don't know or a person who does not identify as male or female.

1 Rewrite the sentence and replace the words in bold with a subject, object or possessive pronoun.

a. **Armie and Plato** vowed never to cook together again.

....

....

b. The Venus flytrap is **the queen's**.

....

c. "That's **mine and Shang High's**!" screamed Brick.

....

....

d. The tractor drove past **Bearnice and Bogart** at lightning speed.

....

....

e. **The girl** hid her brother's tap shoes.

....

f. "It's not my fault! It's **Grit and Brick's**," proclaimed Oz.

....

....

g. **The boat** raced across the river with the stolen jewels onboard.

....

....

h. **The twins** cried for hours after spilling some milk.

....

....

A **relative pronoun** is a **pronoun** that introduces a **relative clause** in a complex sentence. Relative clauses add information about the noun in the main clause.

relative pronoun ⤵

The painting, **which** was hanging on the wall, was painted by Bearnice.

relative clause

Relative pronouns can be **who**, **which**, **whose**, **that**, **where** and **when**.

Who, **which** and **whose** are often used **with a comma**. These relative pronouns often introduce extra information that's not essential for the sentence to make sense, so commas are used to separate the clause.

Relative pronoun	What it refers to	Example sentence
who	people or animals	Bearnice, **who** was going to a costume party, was dressed as a fried egg.
which	animals or things	The loaf of bread, **which** was on fire, was ruined.
whose	people, animals or things in the possessive form	Oz, **whose** birthday was coming up, planned a huge party.

That, **where** and **when** are often used **without a comma**. These relative pronouns often introduce extra information that's essential to make the meaning of the sentence clear.

Relative pronoun	What it refers to	Example sentence
that	people or animals	Armie accidentally ate a sandwich **that** he was allergic to.
where	places	We visited the neighbourhood **where** I used to live.
when	time expressions	I will always remember the day **when** we first met.

1 Draw lines to complete these sentences.

The concert tickets,	**whose** neck is incredibly long,	were from Brick.
Shang High,	**which** Bearnice got for her birthday,	is often blamed for her sister's troublemaking.
Yin,	**who** looks just like Yang,	always hits his head on door frames.

2 Complete these sentences using one of the relative pronouns (who, which, whose, that, where and when) for each sentence.

Say it out loud to make sure it makes sense.

a. This is the library .... Armie spends most of his time.

b. Oz, ... social media account suddenly had over

8 million followers, felt nervous about posting a selfie.

c. The castle, ... was over 500 years old, was falling apart.

d. Shang High only listens to music .... is from the 1980s.

e. The carrot, ... won the world's longest

vegetable competition, was delicious.

People speak in **complex sentences** all the time, but when it comes to writing them down, things can get tricky. When writing complex sentences, there are certain things that you need to watch out for, like when and how to use commas and whether or not to use certain conjunctions (joining words).

A clause is a group of words that contains a verb. Complex sentences consist of a **main clause** and a subordinate clause. The **subordinate clause** is dependent on the main clause, meaning it does not make sense on its own and is used to add extra information to the sentence.

Here are three types of subordinate clauses that can make a complex sentence: **adverbial clauses**, **relative clauses** and **non-finite clauses**.

Let's look at them one by one.

Subordinate clauses that begin with subordinate conjunctions such as **because**, **while**, **even though** or **although** are **adverbial clauses**. This means that they add information about how, why, when or where the action in the main clause takes place.

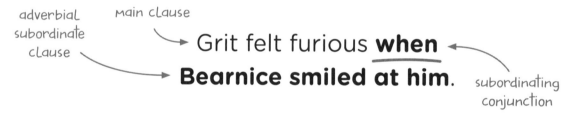

When an adverbial clause goes at the beginning of a sentence, you need to put a comma after it to separate it from the main clause:

TIP!

The subordinate conjunction is always part of the subordinate clause.

1 **Add the missing punctuation and circle the subordinating conjunctions.**

These complex sentences are missing punctuation. Add commas and full stops (where necessary) and then circle the subordinating conjunctions.

a. Oz fainted when she forgot her lines on stage

b. After a long week Bearnice relaxed at a spa

c. Grit chased his tail until he finally caught it

d. After spending all day collecting ingredients
Plato was excited to start cooking

e. When the lights went off everyone started screaming

f. Brick ate two lunches even though he wasn't that hungry

g. Bogart covered his ears whenever Bearnice started to sing

h. After crossing the crumbling bridge
Yin and Yang breathed a sigh of relief

i. Whenever he was lost for words
Shang High felt like his tongue
was tied in a knot

Subordinate clauses that begin with relative pronouns, like **who** or **which**, are called **relative clauses**. Relative clauses add information about the noun in the main clause.

When a relative clause with **who** or **which** goes at the end of a sentence, it needs a comma before it and a full stop after.

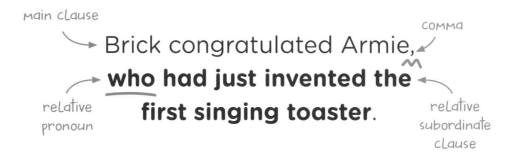

main clause

Brick congratulated Armie,

comma

who had just invented the

relative pronoun

first singing toaster.

relative subordinate clause

When it goes in the middle of the sentence, it needs a comma before it and another comma after it to separate it from the main clause.

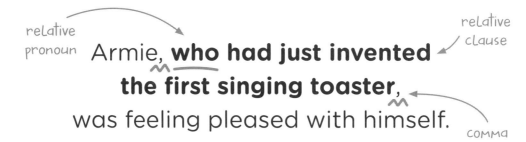

relative pronoun

Armie, **who had just invented**

relative clause

the first singing toaster,

was feeling pleased with himself.

comma

TIP!

Relative clauses should add relevant information that supports the meaning of the sentence.
Good example: Armie, who was very tired, fell asleep instantly.
Bad example: Armie, who is very short, fell asleep instantly.

1 Can you add the correct punctuation to these complex sentences with relative clauses?

Remember, if the relative clause is in the middle of the sentence, it needs a comma before and after. If the relative clause is at the end of the sentence, it needs a comma before it and a full stop after.

a. Shang High who had just put his headphones on was feeling peaceful

TIP!

If you remove the relative clause, the sentence should still make sense.

b. Plato wrote out his grandfather's pancake recipe which had been handed down over four generations

c. Yin angrily chased Yang who had just purposefully smashed her science fair trophy

d. The theme park which had been open for 40 years was closing down

2 Write a relative clause for these complex sentences.

Fill in the gaps with additional information. Remember, the information shared in a relative clause should be relevant to the sentence.

a. Plato, who .... ,

stared longingly at the last piece of cherry pie.

b. The old table, which .... ,

finally collapsed.

c. Grit lost his new watch,

which ....

....

d. Bogart did not fear the fly swatter,

which ....

....

Non-finite clauses add information about the main clause by using a word that ends in **-ing** like **seeing**, **running** or **being**. This type of clause is called non-finite because it doesn't show whether the extra information happened in the past, present or future.

When a non-finite **-ing** clause goes at the beginning of a sentence, it needs a comma after it to separate it from the main clause. When it goes at the end of a sentence, it needs a comma before it. Unlike adverbial clauses, non-finite clauses have a comma separating them from the rest of the sentence, no matter whether they go at the beginning or end.

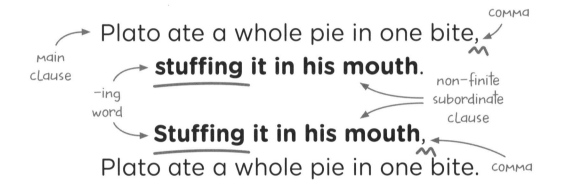

1 Complete the non-finite clauses in these sentences.

Choose the best **-ing** word from below and fill in the blanks. Don't forget to capitalise the first letter if the **-ing** word goes at the beginning of the sentence.

wondering   laughing   stopping

a. Shang High scratched his head, ... what to do next.

b. .... loudly, Bogart watched Brick slip on a banana peel.

c. Armie strolled contentedly around the park,

.... to smell the roses.

Now that we've learned three types of complex sentences,
let's practise using them!

1 **Rewrite these sentences so that the subordinate clause comes first.**
Remember to watch out for where the commas go.

a. Brick crept into the abandoned hotel even though there was a "DANGER" sign on the door.

....

....

....

b. Bogart sat in his underground lair, plotting his next prank.

....

....

2 **Now it's your turn!**
Complete these complex sentences by adding a subordinate clause.
For an extra challenge, see if you can write one **adverbial clause**,
one **relative clause** and one **non-finite -ing clause**! Don't forget to
add commas where necessary.

a. Yin laughed at Yang ....

....

b. ....

.... Grit didn't want to speak to anyone ever again.

c. Armie unlocked the secret door ....

....

The subjunctive is a verb form that is used in formal language to:

1

show the importance
of something being asked

2

express a wish,
desire or hope

TIP!

Formal language is used when writing to people you don't know well
or people you want to show respect to.

When writing in the subjunctive form to show the importance of something
being asked, we use verbs such as **recommend**, **insist**, **demand** and **request**.

I **recommend** that you listen.

He **requests** that they arrive on time.

Oz **demands** that you attend her party.

When expressing something we wish, desire or hope, we use the form **were**.

If I **were** rich, I would buy myself a mansion.

If Oz **were** queen, she would demand
that everyone worship her.

"I wish I **were** able to read
people's minds," thought Armie.

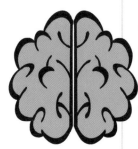

1 Which of these sentences are formal?

Read through these sentences and tick all of the
formal sentences containing the subjunctive form.

a. Oz demanded that the shop give her a refund.

   Oz asked for her money back.

b. Plato thinks that you should try his new recipe.

   Plato recommends that you sample his latest recipe.

c. Shang High requests that you listen to his album.

   Shang High asks everyone he meets to listen to his album.

d. I want to be an environmental scientist when I grow up.

   If I were an environmental scientist, I would clean up the oceans.

2 Now it's your turn!

Help Bearnice write a formal application letter to run for mayor.
Write four formal sentences using the subjunctive form and
the words in bold. The first one has been done for you.

a. **were:** *If I were to be elected as mayor, I would change this
   city for the better.*

b. **recommend:** ....

   ....

c. **request:** ....

   ....

d. **demand:** ....

   ....

PUNCTUATION

When we talk, we use the tone of our voices to make our meaning clear. When we write, we rely on punctuation instead. In this chapter, you'll practise some key punctuation skills to help you make your writing more accurate and more expressive.

Remember that a sentence is a complete idea that makes sense by itself. There are four different types of complete sentences: statements, questions, commands and exclamation sentences.

A **statement** expresses a fact, idea or opinion. This is the most common type of sentence. It usually ends with a full stop and the person or thing doing the action comes before the verb:

Yang loves to cause mischief.

A **question** asks something that needs an answer. It always ends with a question mark. Questions can include any of these features:

1

A question can be marked by **question words**, like **who**, **what**, **when**, **where**, **why** and **how**.

How much longer will it take you to get ready?

A question can **invert** (or switch) the subject and the auxiliary verb, like **be**, **do**, **can** and **have**.

The auxiliary verb comes first to turn this into a question.

The subject comes first in the statement.

You can come to my party tonight.

Can you come to my party tonight?

3

A question can contain a **question tag**. A question tag is added to the end of a statement after a comma. It turns a statement into a question. We use these kinds of questions to find out more information or to confirm that something is true.

You like cheese, **don't you?**

comma

question tag

Plato's a platypus, **isn't he?**

comma

question tag

A **command** tells someone to do something.
It can end with a full stop or an exclamation mark.

Don't go in there!

An **exclamation sentence** tells something with surprise
or strong feeling. It always ends with an exclamation mark.
Exclamation sentences start with **what** or **how**.

What a lovely day it is today!

1 **Read through and label these sentences.**

Label each sentence with an **S** (statement), **Q** (question), **C** (command)
or **E** (exclamation sentence).

a. What is Plato's secret recipe?

b. Leave that sleeping owl alone.

c. Keep the music down!

d. You like puzzles, don't you?

e. How silly Yin and Yang are!

2 **Transform these statements into questions.**

Either invert the subject and verb **or** add a comma and a question tag.

a. Oz is very selfish sometimes.

....

b. Oranges are orange.

....

c. Pigs can't fly.

....

Apostrophes can be used to show contraction or possession.

You can show that something belongs to someone (or something) by using an **apostrophe** and an **-s**.

There are four rules about how you can do this.

You may remember that for most **singular nouns**, we add an **apostrophe** and an **-s**.

That is **Armie's** library card.

It's trickier when **singular nouns end in -s**. In these cases, it is convention that we add an **apostrophe only**.

Today is **James'** birthday.
Texas' temperature is very high in the summer.
The **octopus'** tentacles were very sticky.

When a noun has a **regular plural** (ending in **-s**), to show belonging, you add an **apostrophe only**.

The **boys'** teacher was fluent in seven languages.

However, some **irregular plural nouns** (like one woman, many women) do not end in **-s**. Here, you add an **apostrophe** and an **-s**.

The **women's** department was on the third floor.

1 **Complete these sentences by adding either an apostrophe or an apostrophe and an -s.**

a. Shang High .... scarf could stretch the length of an entire bus.

b. The children .... game became dangerous when it was played on ice.

c. Swans took over the ducks .... favourite puddle.

d. "When was Lucas .... bicycle stolen?" she asked.

e. Food and drink was always central to Plato .... travel plans.

f. She was excellent at remembering people .... names.

g. *Oliver Twist* is one of Charles Dickens .... most famous novels.

h. "Those are Bogart .... blueprints of the city," smiled Bearnice.

The previous examples teach you possession for one noun, but what happens when you have more than one noun in a sentence?

When two or more nouns share ownership of something, the apostrophe and **-s** go on the final noun in the group.

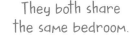

They both share the same bedroom.

Yin and Yang's bedroom is very messy.

That is Oz, Armie and Grit's balloon.

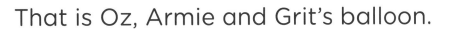

They all share the same balloon.

2 **Rewrite these sentences to include possessive apostrophes.**

The bold sections can be rephrased to include a possessive apostrophe and an **-s**.

a. **The archnemesis of Brick** won the 100m race.

Brick's archnemesis won the 100m race.

b. **The teacher of the children** surprised them with a silent disco.

c. The pineapple trees were planted **by the husband of the mayor**.

d. They all agreed that **the bread of the bakery** was the best bread.

e. **The suit of James** came from the tailors.

f. **The cunning plan of Oz and Bogart** was starting to work.

g. Bearnice couldn't believe her eyes

when she saw **the pose of Yang.**

3 **Write a complete sentence to describe each illustration using a possessive apostrophe.**

You have been given some optional keywords to include in your sentence. The first one has been done for you.

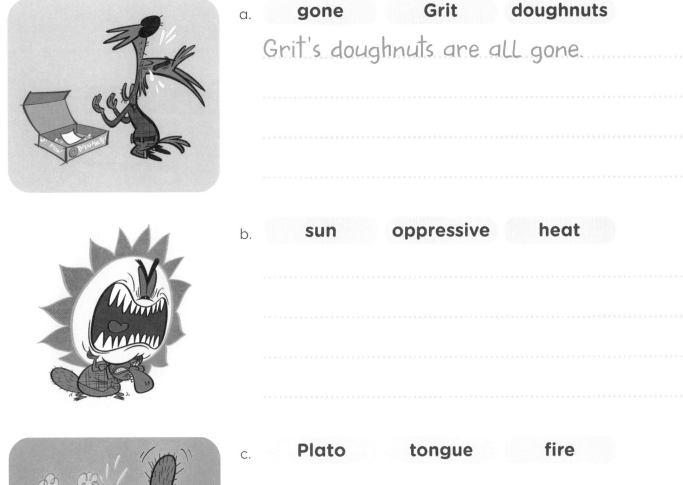

a. | gone | Grit | doughnuts

Grit's doughnuts are all gone.

b. | sun | oppressive | heat

c. | Plato | tongue | fire

d. | the clouds | game | terrifying

Writing with speech can be confusing because we often have a sentence within a sentence. Sometimes, it's helpful to think about the sentence as split into the **speech sentence** and the **real sentence**.

speech sentence   **"I lost my phone!"** cried Oz.   real sentence

The **speech sentence** always starts with a **capital letter** and sits between two **inverted commas**.

DID YOU KNOW?

Inverted commas are also known as speech marks.

Sometimes, the speech sentence comes first. Other times, it comes last.

"That's mine!" screamed Brick.

Speech sentence comes first.

Brick screamed, **"That's mine!"**

Speech sentence comes last.

There is always a punctuation mark before the final inverted comma and this punctuation should be the appropriate type for the speech sentence.

If the speech sentence is a question, use a **question mark**.

"Where do you live**?**" asked Oz.

If the speech sentence is an exclamation sentence, has a strong feeling or is said loudly, use an **exclamation mark**.

"She loves apples**!**" shouted Bearnice.

If the speech sentence is a statement and comes at the **end of the real sentence**, use a **full stop**.

Armie said, "I'd prefer the chicken**.**"

However, if the speech sentence is a statement and comes at the **start of the real sentence**, use a **comma**. You cannot put a full stop at the end of a speech sentence when it's not the end of the real sentence.

"I'd prefer the chicken," said Armie.

When any speech sentence comes at the end of the real sentence, you need to add a comma before it. Remember, the speech sentence always starts with a capital letter.

Grit said, "**L**et's just be quiet for a while."

Oz asked, "**W**here do you live?"

Bearnice shouted, "**S**he loves apples!"

1 Rewrite these sentences by adding punctuation and capital letters where necessary.

Remember to add a comma before the speech if it comes second and that the speech sentence always starts with a capital letter.

a. Bearnice declared this is the worst day of my life

....

b. I can't believe you won cried Brick

....

c. It's not fair moaned Plato

....

d. Oz commanded everyone look at me

....

e. What should I do next pondered Armie

....

Sometimes the part of the sentence that tells you who is speaking can be placed in the middle of a character's speech, splitting the speech sentence into two parts. This is sometimes called **interrupted speech**.

To form these types of sentences, follow these rules:

Inverted commas should be placed around both parts of the speech sentence.

The first part of the speech sentence starts with a capital letter and ends with a comma.

The second part of the speech sentence starts with a lowercase letter and ends with a full stop, exclamation mark or question mark.

The part of the sentence that tells you who is speaking ends with a comma.

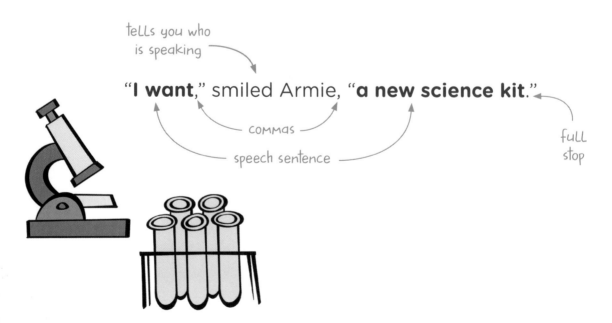

tells you who is speaking

"**I want**," smiled Armie, "**a new science kit**."

commas

speech sentence

full stop

2 **Rewrite these sentences by adding punctuation and capital letters where necessary.**

a. don't snapped Oz touch my phone

b. imagine gasped Shang High a three-week music festival

c. how much questioned Grit is that dinosaur bone

d. I can't admitted Plato eat anymore

e. I shall cackled Bogart tie everyone's shoelaces together

f. I buried the treasure confessed Yang in the back garden

g. I think confessed Brick I might have been working out too much

There are several times you need to remember to use capital letters:

At the **start** of each **sentence**

The toaster is broken.

When writing **I**

My sister and **I** broke the toaster.

At the start of a **speech sentence** (see page 48)

The chef screamed, "**T**he toaster is broken!"

When writing most words in **titles** except the articles, conjunctions and prepositions, unless they come at the start of the title

The **T**errible **T**ale of the **B**roken **T**oaster

When writing a **proper noun** (names of specific people or animals, places or things)

a. Animal names are capitalised when they have a proper noun (often related to location) in their name.

The **G**erman shepherd broke the toaster.

b. Months, days and holidays are capitalised, but seasons aren't.

The toaster was broken before **D**iwali.

The toaster was broken in the summer.

1 Time to get editing!

Some words are missing capital letters and others have incorrect capital letters. Can you fix the capitalisation mistakes? The first one has been done for you.

T
the expedition to the coldest place on the planet was far more gruelling than Bearnice had anticipated. Trekking through the Arctic in the middle of Winter, bearnice hoped to spot a penguin or two (Not realising that penguins do not live in the arctic). She did, however, spot a family of Arctic Foxes, which brightened her frosty mood.

Parentheses (singular: parenthesis) are words, phrases or clauses inserted as **extra information**, an **explanation** or an **afterthought** into a sentence that is grammatically correct and makes sense without it. These usually come directly after the thing they describe and are often separated from the main sentence with brackets, dashes or commas. First, we will focus on **commas**.

The thing the parenthesis describes.

The curry, **which Plato had made without using a recipe,** was delicious.

This underlined sentence makes sense without the parenthesis.

This bolded information is about the curry, but the sentence would still be complete without it.

Commas are usually used to separate parentheses when the writing is formal.

1 **Add the commas around the parentheses in these sentences.**

a. The Arctic fox known for its white fur is able to camouflage itself well in the snow.

b. *Chiroptera* meaning hand wing is the scientific name for bats.

c. Bearnice ate the last and coincidentally biggest slice of cake.

2 **Rewrite these sentences, adding the extra information.**
Remember to add commas around the parentheses.

a. Yin was the teacher's favourite. **known for her excellent behaviour**

....

....

b. The artwork was stolen. **painted by Vincent van Gogh**

....

....

We have seen how commas can be used to separate parentheses from the main sentence. Next, we will focus on parentheses with **brackets**.

This bolded information is about Armie, but the sentence would still be complete without it.

Armie **(an avid reader)** has an extensive library of books.

This underlined sentence makes sense without the parenthesis.

Brackets are used to separate parentheses when you want the extra information to **stand out clearly**. Brackets are a better choice for separating your parentheses than commas when your sentence already uses a lot of commas. Too many commas in one sentence can make it messy and confusing!

Also, you can add **extra punctuation** within the bracketed parenthesis, like an exclamation mark.

Armie **(an avid reader!)** has an extensive library of books.

TIP!

If the brackets go at the end of a sentence, the final punctuation mark goes after the second bracket. For example, "Oz got to the party early (to make sure she had time for selfies)."

1 Add brackets around the parentheses in these sentences.

a. Oz travelled to Paris the capital of France.

b. Grit the grump! disliked everyone.

2 Rewrite this sentence, adding the extra information.
Remember to add brackets around the parentheses.

The attic is full of gadgets.   **which Armie told me never to enter**

We have seen how commas and brackets can be used to separate parentheses from the main sentence. Finally, we will focus on parentheses with **dashes**.

This bolded information is about the brother, but the sentence would still be complete without it.

My brother **– the destroyer –** made a colossal mess of my bedroom.

This underlined sentence makes sense without the parenthesis.

Dashes can be used to separate parentheses when writing **informally** or when trying to emphasise a point in **narrative writing**.

1 **Add dashes around the parentheses in these sentences.**

a. Oz who was in love with herself gazed at her reflection in the mirror.

b. Just then, Grit Plato's friend walked into the room.

c. Bearnice known for her hugs squeezed Bogart way too hard.

2 **Rewrite this sentence, adding the extra information.**
Remember to add dashes around the parentheses.

Grit found a dinosaur bone. **after hours of digging**

....

A sweet smell wafted from the kitchen. **perhaps of cookies or cakes**

....

Shang High paused the music to sneeze. **after four hours of listening**

....

An ellipsis (plural: ellipses) is a punctuation mark consisting of **three dots** (...).

There are different ways an author might choose to use
an ellipsis, including the following:

To **create suspense** by adding a
pause at the end of a sentence.

The door
slowly opened...

To show the **trailing-off** of an
unfinished thought.

"It sounds easy, but..."
Grit began.

To show **where a word or words have been
removed** from a quote to shorten it.

"The Great Wall of China was built by more than six different
Chinese dynasties and is over 2,200 years old."

Main quote   shortened quote

"The Great Wall of China... is over 2,200 years old."

1 **Read each sentence and identify what the
ellipsis is used for.**

Draw lines to match the sentence to the type of ellipsis used.

"I'm not going to..." mumbled Plato.	word or words have been removed
Slowly, they crawled into the dark cave...	unfinished thought
Blue whales... migrate to middle and low altitudes in the winter.	suspense or tension

2 Now it's your turn!

An ellipsis can be a useful tool to use in dramatic writing, but (much like an exclamation mark) it's best not to use it too much. Read through this paragraph and edit the punctuation to add one exclamation mark and one ellipsis to achieve the most dramatic effect.

Plato screamed as he ran from the volcano, doing his best not to fall headfirst into the boiling lava. He'd done it. He had stolen the golden statue, rumoured to contain the legendary apple pie recipe that was lost generations ago. He ran as fast as he could, leaping over crumbling rocks and dodging falling debris, but his biggest concern was behind him. He was convinced someone, or something, was following him.

Colons (:) are commonly used in two ways:

They can be used to link two independent clauses that are closely related. In this sentence, the text after the colon expands on and helps explain or illustrate what comes before it.

Brick exercises often: he goes to the gym three times a day.

They can also be used to introduce a list. In this example, the colon tells us what the two unusual sports were.

Last week, Brick watched two unusual sports: korfball and wheelbarrow racing.

DID YOU KNOW?

What comes before a colon must be a main clause.
What comes after a colon often explains what came before it.

1 Add colons to these sentences.

a. A record amount of snow fell that afternoon it was eight metres deep by 4pm.

b. Plato loves to bake all kinds of treats cakes, pastries and tarts.

c. Shang High is a talented musician he writes all of his own songs.

d. Oz waltzed down the catwalk she had never felt more confident.

e. Grit only ever wanted to be in three places his bed, his armchair or his garden.

Semicolons (;) are commonly used in two ways:

They are used to link two independent clauses that are closely related.
They often stand in for **coordinating conjunctions** like **and** or **but**.

Plato loves cabbage**;** it's his favourite vegetable.

They are also used to separate longer items in lists that
already contain commas or phrases.

Plato tried many different kinds of pizza, including pepperoni,
mozzarella cheese and olives**;** green peppers, meatballs
and onions**;** and even chocolate with marshmallows.

TIP!

Sometimes it can be difficult to decide when to use semicolons and
colons. This often depends on a writer's individual writing style.

1 Add semicolons to these sentences.

a. Yang forgot to lock the back door
Yin hated it when she did that.

b. Oz took a selfie in the garden Bearnice tried
to get to know all the flowers.

c. To make a pie, Plato needs flour, butter and salt for the pastry
plums, apples and sugar for the filling and cherries to decorate.

d. The sailor has been at sea for four months
he writes home to his family every two weeks.

e. Armie built a time machine that could also
bake brownies it was his greatest invention yet.

VOCABULARY

Vocabulary is probably the most important part of learning to read and write with real style. The older you get and the more words you learn, the more you develop your word consciousness. Word consciousness refers to your awareness of the connections between words (like synonyms, antonyms and shades of meaning) as well as how words are built from various parts (like prefixes and suffixes or Greek and Latin roots). Your word consciousness is what empowers you to make the best choices about which words you use in which situations, and to read texts that are full of difficult words with confidence.

Prefixes are a letter or group of letters that are added
to the beginning of words to change their meaning.

The prefix **trans-** means **across**, **through** or **beyond**.

trans + atlantic = transatlantic

meaning to go **across** the Atlantic Ocean

The prefix **bi-** means **two** or **twice**.

bi + cycle = bicycle

meaning a vehicle with **two** wheels

The prefix **semi-** means **half** or **partly**.

semi + circle = semicircle

meaning **half** of a circle

The prefix **tri-** means **three**.

tri + logy = trilogy

meaning **three** related plays, films or novels

① Fill in the blanks.

Complete these sentences by filling in the prefix **trans-**, **bi-**, **tri-** or **semi-**.

a. Bogart secretly ....**ferred** everyone's money into his

own personal account.

b. Yin is ....**lingual** and speaks both English and Mandarin.

c. One of the three legs of Oz's ....**pod** snapped off

and her camera went flying across the room.

d. The cookie recipe called for a dark and sophisticated

.................**sweet** chocolate, but Bearnice paid no attention

and added seven sugary chocolate bars.

② Complete these words.

Add the prefix **trans-**, **bi-**, **tri-** or **semi-** to complete each word.
Then write three sentences, using each completed word once.

a. *n.* any muscle with two points of attachment at one end

............**ceps**

b. *n.* a race involving swimming, cycling and running

............**athlon**

c. *adj.* allowing some light to pass through

............**lucent**

③ Draw lines to match the prefix to the root word.

Say it out loud to make sure it sounds right. As an extra challenge,
try to define each word out loud.

tri	**weekly**
semi	**form**
bi	**angle**
trans	**formal**

Remember that prefixes are a letter or group of letters
that are added to the beginning of words to change their meaning.

The prefix **aero**- relates to the air.

aero + dynamic = aerodynamic

meaning the study of how objects like cars,
planes and helicopters move through the **air**

The prefix **photo**- relates to light.

photo + graph = photograph

meaning a picture taken with a camera using **light**

The prefix **micro**- means small.

micro + scope = microscope

meaning an instrument used to view **small** things

The prefix **tele**- means distant or at a distance.

tele + scope = telescope

meaning an instrument used to make
distant objects look larger

1 ## Complete these words.

Add the prefix **aero**-, **photo**-, **micro**-
or **tele**- to complete each word.
Say it out loud to make sure
it sounds right.

a. ....vision

b. ....grapher

c. ....chip

d. ....nautical

2 Transform these sentences with the right prefix!

Pick the correct prefix and write the whole word in the gap to complete the sentence. Say it out loud to make sure it sounds right.

a. Oz dreamed of starring in a reality show where her every

word would be ....

photo **tele** vised

b. Armie's latest invention worked perfectly for half

a ...., after which it promptly exploded.

tele **micro** second

c. The process by which plants use light, water and carbon

dioxide to produce nutrients is called ....

photo **aero** synthesis

d. Yin and Yang spent all afternoon ....

their paws and tails.

micro **photo** copying

e. If he wanted to build a rocket,

Armie would first need to

master ....

engineering.

aero **photo** space

Some words are made up of different parts, such as **prefixes** (a letter or group of letters added to the beginning of a word), **suffixes** (a letter or group of letters added to the end of a word) and **roots**. The root is the main part of the word and carries the meaning.

Many root words, prefixes and suffixes in the English language originate from Greek and Latin. Understanding what these mean can help you work out the meaning of a word in English.

For example, the Greek root word **chron** means **time**.

chronological

adj. arranged in
the order of **time**

chronometer

n. an instrument used
for measuring **time**

From now on, if you ever see a word with **chron**, you will know that it is probably related to the Greek root word and means something to do with **time**.

TIP!

When we notice things like root words, prefixes and suffixes, it helps develop our word consciousness. This is our awareness of words that helps us to spell and learn new vocabulary.

---

1 **Recognising different parts of a word is the perfect skill for a vocabulary detective.**
Let's get practising!

a. The Greek root **geo** means earth.
The Greek suffix **logy** means the study of.
What do you think **geology** means?

....

b. The Greek root **dem** means people.
The Greek suffix **cracy** means power.
What do you think **democracy** means?

....

c. The Latin root **pac** means peace.
The Latin suffix **ify** means to make or cause to be.
What do you think **pacify** means?

....

d. The Greek root word **acro** means height.
The Greek root word **phobia** means fear.
What does it mean if a person is **acrophobic**?

....

2 Let's practise more!

Read the "evidence" and draw your conclusion about
what each root word means.

a. An **anti**dote is a remedy that works against a poison.
Antiwar means to be opposed to or against war.
What do you think **anti** means?

....

b. A **burs**ar is someone who looks after money.
A **burs**ary is a sum of money given to someone.
What do you think **burs** means?

....

c. In**cred**ulous means not believing something.
A **cred**it card is a bank card that allows you to spend
money that the bank believes you can and will pay back.
What do you think **cred** means?

....

d. **Prim**itive relates to human society in its first stages of development.
A **prim**er is a substance used on metal or wood first, before adding paint.
What do you think **prim** means?

....

Homophones are words that sound the same but differ in meaning and spelling. A near homophone is a word that sounds almost the same as another word but differs in meaning and spelling.

1 **Circle the correct homophone to complete these sentences.**

a. "I hate ketchup!" yelled Grit as he (**threw**) (**through**) his sandwich on the ground.

b. Bearnice ate the last (**peace**) (**piece**) of cake.

c. "Are you going to space (**two**) (**to**) (**too**) ?" asked Armie.

d. Oz bought herself a (**pair**) (**pear**) of stylish sunglasses.

e. "I didn't (**no**) (**know**) the test was today!" gulped Brick.

f. "You're the (**guessed**) (**guest**) of honour!" cried Bearnice.

Here are some examples of homophones and near homophones that you might not be familiar with.

isle *(n.)* an island

aisle *(n.)* a narrow space between rows of seats

draft *(n.)* a non-final version of a piece of text or art

draught *(n.)* a current of cold air in a room or confined space

serial *(adj.)* part of or taking place in a series

cereal *(n.)* food made from grains and eaten with milk

descent *(n.)* a downward movement

dissent *(n.)* a strong difference in opinion

devise *(v.)* to plan or invent something

device *(n.)* an object invented for a specific purpose

who's *(pronoun)* contraction of who is or who has

whose *(pronoun)* belonging to someone or something

2 Complete the sentences with the correct homophone.

Some of these are listed above, so you can use those definitions to help you if you need.

aisle / isle   descent / dissent   weight / wait

draft / draught   write / right   cereal / serial

a. The supermarket was so huge it had

a whole .... dedicated to canned beans.

Grit dreamed of living on his own private ....,

as far away from other people as possible.

b. Brick had to .... three days for the next train home.

Grit's knees buckled under the .... of four heavy boxes.

c. After months of work, Armie had finally finished

the first .... of his book.

Bearnice shivered as she felt a ....

come in through the open window.

d. The longest running .... drama

has been on television for over 80 years.

Grit's favourite breakfast .... is

a bowl of extra small bones and milk.

e. Oz decided to .... a letter to

her favourite person – her future self.

"The haunted basement is down the stairs

and on the ....," said the tour guide.

f. "Please fasten your seatbelts. This plane is about

to begin its ....," announced the pilot.

Bogart was a ruthless leader and did

not tolerate .... from his subjects.

3 **Complete the sentences.**
Fill the blanks with **device** or **devise**.

TIP!
Device is a noun and devise is
a verb. This can be quite tricky,
so think about what the word is
doing in the sentence. Is it
a verb or a noun?

a. The spy used a special ....

to track the movements of her target.

b. Bogart began to .... a plan to take over the world using a

single jar of pickles.

c. Oz's main objective of the day was to .... a strategy to gain more social media followers.

d. Armie invented a life-saving .... but accidentally dropped it in a lake.

e. Shang High uses an app to .... his famous party playlists.

4 Complete the sentences.

Fill the blanks with **whose** or **who's**.

> **TIP!**
>
> Whose and who's are both pronouns, but whose is a possessive pronoun and who's is a contraction of "who is" or "who has". This can be quite tricky, so try reading the sentence out loud with the expanded form of "who is" or "who has" to see if it makes sense.

a. "........................... bones are these?" asked Grit with a sly smile.

b. "........................... going to clean up my mess?" demanded Oz.

c. Bearnice wasn't sure .... playlist this was, so she complimented everyone at the party just in case.

d. "........................... knocking at the door at 2am?!" grumbled Brick.

e. "As soon as we find out .... fingerprints these are, the case will be closed!" announced the detective.

Synonyms are words that mean the same or nearly
the same as another word. When you want to be more precise,
choosing the right synonym is an excellent way to do it.

1 Match the synonyms!

Draw lines to match the words to their corresponding synonyms.

hate	fatigued
huge	loathe
beautiful	enormous
sleepy	scenic

2 Complete these sentences with a suitable synonym.

Read through these sentences and fill in the gaps with a synonym that matches
the word in brackets.

wicked	vivid	innovative

a. Bogart's .... (evil) plan was finally coming together!

b. Yang came up with a truly ....(creative) way to avoid
cleaning her room.

c. Shang High has a .... (colourful) imagination.

③ Upgrade this story.

Cross out the words in bold and replace them with a synonym.
Use the words listed below or challenge yourself and choose your own!

grinned	**intrepid**	**pensive**	**finest**
devious	**wise**	**boisterous**	**unlimited**

Oz was famous for hosting the most **lively** costume

parties ever. So when a distinctively pink envelope

arrived at Bearnice's door, she knew who it was from

immediately. The note read, "Party. Tonight. Wear your **best** outfit."

Bearnice squealed with excitement and set to work on her outfit.

The costume possibilities were **endless**! She could be **a brave** astronaut,

or **a cunning** pirate or something no one had ever seen or thought of

before like… **a thoughtful** hotdog? In the end, Bearnice settled for

something a little more magical – **a knowledgeable** wizard.

Incredibly pleased with herself, Bearnice **smiled** as she entered the

party. She was the only one wearing a costume! The whole party fell

silent until Yang cried, "We can wear costumes? Be right back!"

Seconds later, Yang re-entered the room dressed as the most

philosophical hotdog Bearnice had ever seen.

An antonym is a word that means the opposite of another word.
For example, **happy** and **sad** are antonyms.

4 Find the antonyms!

Draw lines to match the illustrations to the words that best describe them,
then draw lines from those words to their corresponding antonyms.

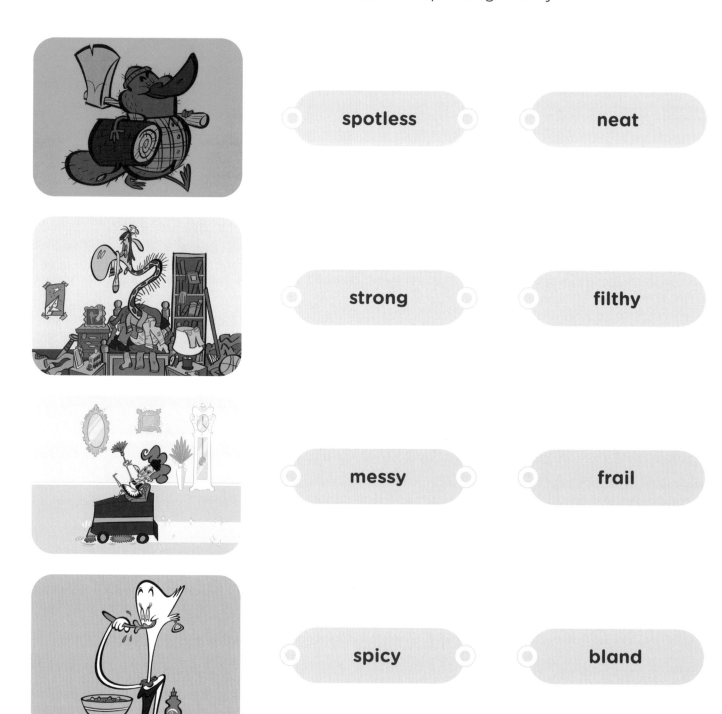

spotless   neat

strong   filthy

messy   frail

spicy   bland

5 Complete the sentences with a suitable antonym.

Read through these sentences and fill in the gaps with an antonym that matches the word in brackets.

a. Oz looked in the mirror with a .... **(modest)** grin on her face.

b. Bearnice hosted a .... **(meagre)** New Year's Eve party.

c. Oz was .... **(impressed)** with her new dress. It didn't match any of her shoes!

d. Brick wrote a .... **(insincere)** apology letter after forgetting Bearnice's birthday.

e. Bearnice woke up feeling .... **(lazy)**.

f. Bogart made a .... **(private)** announcement that he was running for mayor.

g. Bogart believed that he was .... **(inferior)** to everyone else.

Remember, choosing the right synonym is an excellent way to be more precise. Some synonyms have similar meanings, but one is stronger than the other. This is called shades of meaning.

The cheese is **smelly**.
The rotten eggs are **stinking**.
Plato's breath is **putrid**.

The words putrid and stinking both have similar meanings to **smelly**, but you might use **putrid** when you are talking about really, really smelly things. Here, **putrid** is stronger than **stinking**.

1 **Complete the table.**

Each word in the table has two synonyms listed below. The two synonyms have similar meanings but one is stronger than the other.

colossal   adore   attractive   inconsolable   ~~tiny~~   ~~microscopic~~

content   huge   stunning   overjoyed   miserable   idolise

word	synonym	stronger synonym
small	tiny	microscopic
big		
happy		
sad		
beautiful		
love		

2 Which sentence uses the strongest synonym?

Read the sentences and answer the questions. These synonyms may have the same or similar meanings, but one is stronger than the other.

a. **Grit was angry.**

Brick was irate.

Who was angrier?

....

b. **Paris is freezing.**

London is chilly.

Which city is colder?

....

c. **Shang High found the lesson boring.**

Bogart thought it was tedious.

Who had a worse time in the lesson?

....

d. **Bearnice carefully sorted her records.**

Oz rigorously organised her records.

Who was more thorough?

....

e. **Roller coasters make Shang High feel excited.**

Roller coasters make Plato feel exhilarated.

Who enjoyed the roller coaster ride more?

....

Shades of meaning aren't always about using a stronger or weaker synonym, they're also about the context (situation or circumstance).

Brick was given the **laborious** task of pushing an enormous boulder up a mountain.

Armie was stuck inside for days, making his way through **tedious** paperwork.

Laborious and **tedious** have similar meanings, but laborious usually refers to a task that is physically tiring and tedious refers to something boring. We call these subtle differences in meaning **nuances**.

TIP!

It often helps to consider whether a word has positive or negative connotations.

First, look at these synonyms and their definitions. Can you spot the ways in which they are similar and the ways in which they are different?

stubborn

adj. refusing to give in; like someone who has lost an argument but won't admit it

VS

determined

adj. decided and purposeful; like someone who doesn't stop running before the finishing line

tongue-tied

adj. nervous and lost for words; like not being able to speak when you feel shy

VS

speechless

adj. shocked and lost for words; how you feel when someone hangs up on you

cunning

adj. sly and crafty;
like someone who cleverly
gets out of doing their chores

astute

adj. clever or quick-witted;
like someone who understands
things quickly

1 **Complete these sentences with the most appropriate synonym.**

Remember, both synonyms will make sense in each sentence but one will be better suited than the other.

a. Grit was feeling .... and

refused to get out of bed.

Bearnice was .... to reach the

top of the mountain.

stubborn

determined

b. Oz was utterly .... when her

telephone turned into a banana.

When Armie walked on stage, he became

completely ....

tongue-tied

speechless

c. It was Bogart's .... idea to

swap the sugar and the salt.

When Armie finished the book, he made some

.... observations.

cunning

astute

SPELLING

Using the correct spelling of a word helps your reader understand exactly what you mean. In this chapter, you'll master some challenging spelling rules, some spelling variations of common endings and some commonly misspelled words.

When the **shus sound** comes at the end of a word, it can be spelled in two different ways.

-cious
malicious

-tious
nutritious

Sometimes, the spelling of the root word can help us figure out which spelling to use.

If the root word ends in **-ce**, we often use **-cious**.

gra**ce** → gra**cious**

If the root word ends in **-tion**, we often use **-tious**.

ambi**tion** → ambi**tious**

Watch out! There are many exceptions to these rules, but they can still be useful to keep in mind.

TIP!

The shus sound is often found in adjectives (describing words).

1 ## Circle the correct spelling of the words in bold.

Remember to think about the root word to help you figure it out.

a. Grit made up a   fictitious   ficticious

story about battling a robot lizard.

b. Democracy was a   contencious   contentious   subject for Bogart

and his plans for world domination.

2 ## Complete these sentences.

Fill in the blanks with words ending in **-cious** or **-tious**, using the root word to help you.

a. Bogart's evil lair was very .... **(space)**

b. Yin is more .... than her sister. **(caution)**

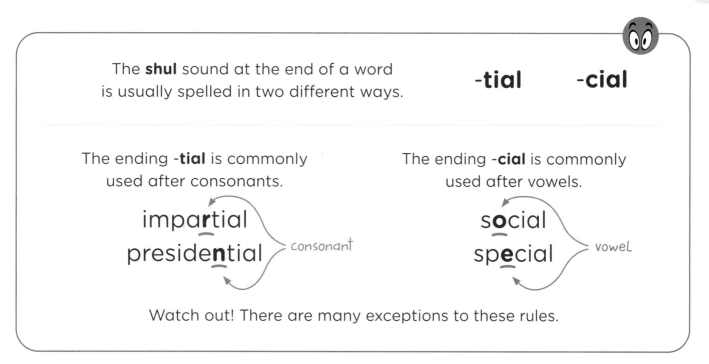

The **shul** sound at the end of a word
is usually spelled in two different ways.

-tial   **-cial**

The ending **-tial** is commonly
used after consonants.

impa**r**tial
preside**n**tial ⟩ consonant

The ending **-cial** is commonly
used after vowels.

s**o**cial
sp**e**cial ⟩ vowel

Watch out! There are many exceptions to these rules.

① Circle the correct spelling of the words in bold.
Remember to look at the letter before the suffix to help you decide
which ending is correct.

a. Bogart's favourite places to wreak havoc are quiet,

residencial   **residential**   areas.

b. Plato's red velvet cupcakes are so delicious that they can

have a   **benefitial**   **beneficial**   effect on your health.

c. Yang was given an   **official**   **offitial**   warning

after her cactus prank went too far.

② Now it's your turn!
Complete these words with **-tial** or **-cial** and use it to write a sentence.

a. **gla**................   *adj.* extremely cold or icy

....

b. **confiden**................   *adj.* intended to be kept private

....

Sometimes words ending in
-able and **-ible** can sound similar.
These words are usually **adjectives**.

Sometimes words ending in
-ably and **-ibly** can also sound similar.
These words are usually **adverbs**.

ador**able**

poss**ible**

ador**ably**

poss**ibly**

TIP!

The suffixes –able and –ible usually mean "capable of being or doing something".

The **-able** suffix is typically used
when a **complete root word** can
be heard before the suffix.

The **-ible** suffix is typically used
when a **stem** comes before the suffix
and not a complete root word.

For example, in the word **likeable**, you
can hear the complete root word **like**.

For example, in the word **audible**,
aud is not a complete root word.

1 ## Add the suffix -able or -ible to complete these words.

Remember the **-able** suffix is typically added to a complete root word
and the **-ible** suffix is typically added to an incomplete root word.

a. incred............   c. laugh............   e. comfort............   g. respons............

b. poss............   d. consider............   f. notice............   h. vis............

2 ## Complete the table.

Underline the **-able**, **-ible**, **-ably** and **-ibly** suffixes in each word in the box.
Then, write the words under the matching spelling pattern.

miserably	agreeable	visibly	responsible

-able	-ible	-ably	-ibly

3 **Read through the story and add the -able, -ible,**
-ably or -ibly suffix to complete the words in bold.

Watch out for the word's function in the sentence to help you decide. If it is an
adjective, it will end in -**able** or -**ible**. If it is an adverb, it will end in -**ably** or -**ibly**.

Grit took a lot of pride in his gardening. Over the years, he'd won many

awards for his **incred**................... petunias and awe-inspiring bonsai

trees. He was a **respons**................... gardener too, always making sure

to water his plants when they needed it. Then, last year, something

shocking happened. Armie won every single gardening award on offer.

"It's not fair! He's cheating!" Grit pouted **miser**.................. Armie's

garden used all the latest gardening technology. If Grit wanted to win

an award ever again, he was going to have to do the same.

Over the next months, Grit spent a **consider**................... amount of

time perfecting his futuristic garden – 900 hours, to be precise. He was

vis................... exhausted, but it was worth it. He had created a garden

that most people wouldn't think **poss**.............. until at least the year

3050 and he was starting to act a little smug about it.

"Wow, is that an artificially intelligent

robot gardener?" gawked Bearnice

as she passed by.

"Huh? Oh, that old thing?" Grit replied.

"Yeah, I didn't think it was that

notice................."

Sometimes, words ending in **-ant** and **-ent** sound the same but are spelled differently.

hesit**ant**
innoc**ent**

both endings are pronounced "unt"

1 Complete the table.

Underline the **-ant** and **-ent** endings in each word in the box. Then, write the words under the matching spelling pattern.

repellent   dominant

vacant   present

independent   significant

assistant   radiant

argument   resident

president   brilliant

-ant	-ent

2 Circle the correct spelling of the words in bold.

a. The house at the end of the street had been   **vacant**   **vacent**   for many years.

b. Some people call Oz loud and selfish, but she says she simply has a   **dominent**   **dominant**   personality.

c. Bogart always dreamed of being   **presidant**   **president**   .

d. Yin yearned to be a little more   **independant**   **independent**   from her sister.

e. Armie spent a **significicent** **significant** amount of time every day reading.

3 Complete the words in bold by adding -ant or -ent.

a. "I need my own personal **assist**................," demanded Oz.

b. Yang always starts the **argum**................, but Yin always wins it.

c. Bearnice loved spending hours finding the perfect **pres**................ for her friends' birthdays.

4 Read this story.

Fill in the blanks with the correct words ending in **-ant** and **-ent**.

brilliant	repellent	resident	president

No one had ever seen the .... of number 35 Bollard Street. Some rumours said she was a ...., award-winning journalist who was working on a top-secret story. Other rumours said she was the former .... of a far-off country and was now in hiding, deep undercover. Either way, she definitely did not want any visitors. This was made perfectly clear by the forest of cacti around her gate, which appeared to act as a .... to anyone trying to reach the doorbell.

Sometimes words ending in -**ance** and -**ence** can sound similar. So can words ending in -**ancy** and -**ency**.

These words often have root words ending in -**ant** and -**ent**.

relev**ant** ➔ relev**ance**

inf**ant** ➔ inf**ancy**

pati**ent** ➔ pati**ence**

consist**ent** ➔ consist**ency**

TIP!

Saying the word how it is spelled (and exaggerating each sound) can help you remember the difference.

1 Transform these words into their forms ending in -ence or -ance.

a. attendant ➔ ....

b. tolerant ➔ ....

c. diligent ➔ ....

d. prominent ➔ ....

e. resident ➔ ....

f. evident ➔ ....

2 Transform these words into their forms ending in -ency or -ancy.

a. vacant ➔ ....

b. decent ➔ ....

3 Read through the story and fill in the gaps with the transformed words from questions 1 and 2.

Ever since Oz had taken up ....

on Aviary Road, she'd had terrible luck.

Truly dreadful, awful luck. Her garden furniture

was carried away by a group of cunning swans,

her hot tub was used as a giant owls' nest and her

hair extensions were stolen by a flock of bald eagles.

Some said Oz was falsely accusing these birds,

but she had ....: mainly the fact that the bald eagles weren't so bald anymore. But this was not the worst crime that Oz fell victim to. Worst of all was that the local birds had taken to using Oz's car as a bathroom and her .... was wearing thin. "These birds have no sense of ....!" Oz cried, shaking her fists at the sky.

Oz tried everything to stop them. She parked her car on a different street, but the birds still found it. She stayed up late guarding her car with ...., but the birds pounced as soon as she dozed off. She even hosted an all-night party, at which all birds in the neighbourhood were in .... Surely that would distract them. But at the end of the night, as they headed home, the birds all took a quick detour to visit Oz's car. Disgusting.

Oz knew she only had one choice left. If her car was going to be the neighbourhood bathroom, she was going to have to embrace it. If she played her cards right and used her social media skills, her car might rise to worldwide ....

Oz got to work immediately, hoping she might soon be the proud owner of the most famous toilet in history.

The /ee/ sound is most often spelled with **ee** or **ea**, but it can also be spelled **ie** or **ei**. Remembering whether the **i** or the **e** goes first can be difficult. Luckily, there's a helpful little rhyme you can use to help you:

i before e except after a soft c

Remember! A soft **c** sounds like **s** as in city, cent, face.

So, in a word like **piece**, the **i** comes first. But in the word **deceive**, because the /ee/ sound is after a soft **c**, the **e** comes first.

TIP!

Annoyingly, the "i before e except after a soft c" rule doesn't always work! It can be helpful a lot of the time, but you need to be aware of the exceptions, like "weird", "protein" and "seize".

1 **Circle the correct spellings of the words in bold.**

Remember, **i** before **e** except after a soft **c**!

a. Oz waltzed on stage to ⬭ recieve ⬭ ⬭ receive ⬭ her award.

b. Bogart worked hard to ⬭ achieve ⬭ ⬭ acheive ⬭ world domination.

c. Bearnice accidentally ate the last ⬭ peice ⬭ ⬭ piece ⬭ of Brick's birthday cake.

d. "Alone at last," Grit said with a sigh of ⬭ relief ⬭ ⬭ releif ⬭ .

e. Yang had once again successfully ⬭ deceived ⬭ ⬭ decieved ⬭ her sister.

f. Grit is very well trained and can ⬭ retrieve ⬭ ⬭ retreive ⬭ any ball, no matter how far it's thrown.

g. Oz is so **conceited** **concieted** that she posts

a selfie on social media every four and a half minutes.

② Read the passage below.
Fill in the blanks with the correct **ie** and **ei** words.

| inconceivable | receipts | chief | thieves |

Bogart had no interest in making friends. He firmly believed that

at no point in history had a friend ever been helpful to anyone, ever.

And he had the .... to prove it. Bearnice always

looked on the bright side of his evil schemes, Armie always pointed

out his spelling mistakes and Oz constantly insulted his outfits. It was

.... to Bogart that a friend would ever be useful in

the slightest, until he saw Yin and Yang working together. The duo

were master ...., using teamwork to make sure they

were never caught by the .... detective. "Huh,"

Bogart thought to himself. "Guess it's time to make some friends."

Some words are a little trickier to spell than others.
These words don't follow the rules we expect them to follow.

Some people call these exception words.
We call them **rebel words**.

These are words we have to learn by heart
and it can be fun to practise them in different ways.

1 Copy out these rebel words.

Underline the tricky parts of these spellings. Copy out each rebel word three times and read it aloud. Extra challenge! Try not to look at the original word the third time you write it out.

> **TIP!**
> Sometimes saying the word how it's spelled can be a helpful way to remember it.

a. awkward

b. stomach

c. foreign

d. determined

e. interrupt

f. immediately

g. desperate

h. persuade

i. mischievous

j. embarrass

2 Circle the correct spelling in each sentence.

a. Armie let out an **awkward** **akward** laugh.

b. Plato wanted his food delivery to arrive **imediately** **immediately** .

c. Bogart was **desparate** **desperate** to win.

d. Yang always tried to **embarras** **embarrass** her sister.

e. "Don't **interrupt** **interupt** me!" shouted Bogart.

3 Complete the sentences.
Choose the correct spelling and fill in the blanks.

stumac / stomach   **foren / foreign**   **persuade / perswade**

mischievous / mischivous   **determined / determind**

a. Grit's .... rumbled loudly.

b. Plato dreamed of travelling to ....

lands and tasting every culture's food.

c. Recently, Yang had been more .... than usual.

d. Bogart tried to .... the city that he would make

an excellent mayor.

e. Plato was .... to run a marathon, no matter what.

READING AND WRITING

Here, you will read character-rich fiction texts and illuminating non-fiction texts. You will answer some questions about the text and some questions that ask you to practise skills that you learned in the rest of the book. At the end of some sections, there are prompts to help you take your writing to the next level.

In this section, we're going to focus on reading comprehension skills when reading **fiction** texts. Reading comprehension is all about reading a text carefully, taking your time and understanding it.

Here, we'll be reading the Mrs Wordsmith version of an **Anansi story**.

Anansi stories are folktales that originated in West Africa, with the most well known believed to be from Ghana. The protagonist, Anansi, is a cunning trickster, who uses wit and creativity to get his way in these moral tales. Anansi's name comes from the Akan word for spider and in the stories he often takes the form of a spider. Anansi is often thought of as the god of stories and our retelling of **Anansi and the Snake** explores how he earns this title.

These types of folktales belong to the oral tradition of storytelling. This means that they were often passed on from generation to generation through the spoken word, instead of written down. The characters and the plot remained generally the same over time, but other details were added or taken away depending on the storyteller. It is believed that Anansi stories spread from West Africa to the Caribbean through the transatlantic slave trade from the 16th to the 19th century. These stories were often a symbol of resistance against slave owners as Anansi repeatedly defeats his oppressors using his wit and creativity.

Before we read the Mrs Wordsmith retelling of **Anansi and the Snake**, let's take a look at some vocabulary to get us in the mood.

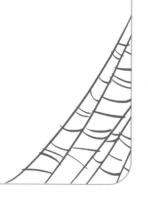

lavish

adj. sumptuous and luxurious;
like a huge banquet for
just one person

WORD PAIRS

lavish **banquet**
lavish **gift**
lavish **lifestyle**

tranquil

adj. peaceful or blissfully quiet;
like how you feel when you take
a nap in the shade

WORD PAIRS

tranquil **surroundings**
tranquil **garden**
tranquil **atmosphere**

treacherous

adj. dangerous or unsafe;
like terrifying rapids that
throw your boat around

WORD PAIRS

treacherous **journey**
treacherous **water**
treacherous **road**

sheepish

adj. shy, ashamed or uncomfortable; like feeling too nervous to go on stage

WORD PAIRS

sheepish **grin**
sheepish **laugh**
sheepish **apology**

reverberating

adj. echoing and vibrating; like crashing cymbals that shake your whole body

WORD PAIRS

reverberating **crash**
reverberating **echo**
reverberating **explosion**

scorn

adj. dislike and contempt; like how an environmentalist feels when they see littering

WORD PAIRS

bitter scorn
public scorn
utmost scorn

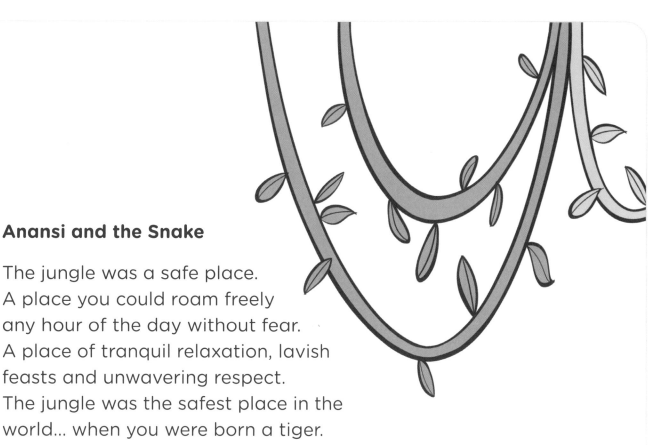

Anansi and the Snake

The jungle was a safe place.
A place you could roam freely
any hour of the day without fear.
A place of tranquil relaxation, lavish
feasts and unwavering respect.
The jungle was the safest place in the
world... when you were born a tiger.

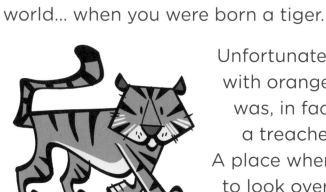

Unfortunately, for all those not blessed
with orange and black stripes, the jungle
was, in fact, quite the opposite. It was
a treacherous and hostile environment.
A place where you were constantly forced
to look over your shoulder. A place of
deceit, betrayal and desperation.

Everything in the jungle belonged to Tiger. The trees were hers, the
fruit was hers, the thin layer of dewy moss on the rocks was hers,
even the breeze was hers. But Anansi didn't long for any of those
things. He longed for Tiger's stories.

Anansi was about one inch tall and
three inches wide, with eight thin,
wiry legs. He lived a solitary life
and most of the other animals
barely cast him a second glance.
When they did notice him, they
simply referred to him as "a spider".

"Urgh, there goes a spider," Buffalo would spit with scorn, mid-mouthful, before returning to her dinner. "A" spider, not even "the" spider. To them, Anansi was nothing but one in tens of thousands of others exactly the same as him.

One afternoon, around the same time as Sloth's daily nap, Anansi decided to take matters into his own hands and ask Tiger for a favour.

"Tiger!" he called into the darkness, "You have it all – admiration, respect, fear – and deservedly so. I didn't come to ask for any of that. I came to ask for your stories. You see, if the jungle's stories were named after me, Anansi, everyone might finally know my name. I am hoping you are as generous as you are brave…"

"…and… beautiful?" he added after a moment's silence for good measure.

From the darkness echoed a deep, reverberating chuckle. Anansi gulped. The laughter spread quickly in all directions and before Anansi could say, "Never mind, so sorry, have a nice day," he was face to face with Tiger.

"The audacity of this creature to make such a request," whispered Tiger to herself. There was no way she was going to give up her precious stories to someone as insignificant and pathetic as a spider… but that didn't mean she couldn't have some fun first.

"Oh spider, of course you can have my stories," she smirked. "If you can capture Snake."

Tiger howled with laughter, but Anansi wasn't sure he understood the joke. "Snake? The seven-metre-long, bloodthirsty python? Will do!" he called gleefully as he skittered away from the pack. This seemed to make Tiger laugh even harder, but Anansi decided that it was best not to dwell on it too much – he had work to do.

The next three days were a process of trial and error. At first Anansi kept things simple, digging deep pits for Snake to fall into and setting up huge nets to scoop Snake up. But when these traditional methods failed, Anansi quickly found his techniques getting more and more desperate. Most shameful was the time he dressed up as a gorgeous boa constrictor to lure Snake towards a trapdoor. Anansi would rather we didn't focus too much on that afternoon.

On the fourth day, Anansi had a realisation. He'd been trying methods beyond his skillset. Perhaps Mole would be able to dig deep pits or Gorilla would be strong enough to hoist Snake up in a net, but not a spider. A spider is cunning, a spider is a trickster and this spider knew exactly what to do next.

"Snake!" he called into the darkness, "Mouse told me that Gorilla told him that Flamingo said to Elephant that you are not longer than this stick of bamboo!"

"That'ssss clearly a lie!" hissed Snake, slithering into the light. "I am much, much longer than any pathetic ssssstick of bamboo."

"Oh, really? That's not what Orangutan said. She said that Hippo told her that Rhinoceros thinks you must be shrinking with old age," replied Anansi innocently.

"Right, let'ssssss put an end to this nonsssssenssse," scowled Snake. She slithered alongside the stick of bamboo to measure her lengthy body.

"How about I tie your tail to one end of the stick so that no one can accuse you of cheating?" offered Anansi helpfully.

"Yessss pleasssse," replied Snake, desperate to squash any senseless rumours.

"And I'll tie your head too for good measure," added Anansi.

"Good idea, thanksssss," nodded Snake.

And just like that, without her even realising, Anansi had captured Snake. Animals from all across the jungle gathered to marvel at the sight. "Ssssee, I'm much longer than this sssssstick! Take that, Flamingo! Who'ssss short now, Hippo! Hah!" sang Snake gleefully. Amongst the gathering crowd stood a rather sheepish-looking Tiger. Anansi beamed at her.

"So," he grinned, gesturing to Snake smugly. "About those stories…"

1 Why do you think the jungle
was a safe place for tigers?

....

....

....

2 How can you tell that the other animals did
not respect Anansi at the start of the story?
Copy one quote from the text.

....

....

....

3 Why do you think Anansi said this to Tiger?

"...and... beautiful?" he added after a moment's silence for good measure.

....

....

4 Based on the context of this quote,
what do you think **audacity** means?

"The audacity of this creature to make such a request,"
whispered Tiger to herself.

....

....

5 There is one point in the story where the author directly addresses the reader (paragraph 13).

   a. Can you underline it?

   b. What do you think the effect or benefit of this direct address is?

....

....

....

6 Why did Anansi's first attempts at capturing Snake fail?

....

....

7 Why did Anansi reference so many animals when talking to Snake?

....

....

8 In this quote, Anansi is not actually being **helpful**. Why do you think the author might have chosen to use this word anyway?

"How about I tie your tail to one end of the stick so that no one can accuse you of cheating?" offered Anansi **helpfully**.

....

....

9 Why do you think Snake cared about being longer than a stick of bamboo? In your answer, include two adjectives to describe her personality.

....

....

....

10 This sentence from the final paragraph is not very descriptive. Can you rewrite it as three sentences to include more detail?

Animals from all across the jungle gathered to marvel at the sight.

....

....

....

....

....

....

....

....

....

....

....

....

In this section, we are going to focus on reading comprehension skills when reading **science fiction** texts.

Science fiction is a genre of storytelling that typically explores an imagined future, especially one that is technologically or scientifically advanced.

First, we will look at some vocabulary that will help you when you read the story.

Once you have read through these words, you'll be ready to read the story called **Exit Game**.

Then, use the text to help you answer the questions. If you aren't sure about an answer, go back and read the text again.

Finally, it's your turn! Time to write your own science fiction story introduction.

extravagant

adj. **excessive or over the top**

The billionaire hosted extravagant dinner parties that lasted 3 days.

retro

adj. **of a similar style to the past**

The costume party had a retro 1960s theme.

condemned

adj. **sentenced to a particular punishment**

She was condemned to a month of detention after starting a vicious food fight.

disembodied

adj. **seemingly not connected to a body**

A disembodied voice whispered softly through the wall.

counterfeit

adj. **made to look exactly like the original of something**

The criminal made over £8 million pounds selling counterfeit paintings.

nimble

adj. **able to move quickly and with precision**

The small but nimble boxer defeated the heavyweight champion.

Exit Game

There were plenty of words you wouldn't use to describe Oz. Shy was one. Humble was another. Generous, thoughtful and considerate were a few more. Everyone knew Oz was a self-obsessed social media fanatic with an attitude problem.

However, what people didn't know about Oz was that she spoke three languages, loved to paint and was the highest-ranked racing driver on a retro video game called *Furiously Fast*. This hand-held car-racing game had outdated graphics that hadn't been impressive since 1980, but Oz loved it. She knew by heart the name of every car and every twist and turn of every racetrack. So when the sequel, *Furiously Fast: Even Faster*, was released as a virtual reality game, Oz simply had to play it.

Technology had advanced beyond Oz's wildest dreams since the release of the original game, with flying cars and robot personal assistants being the top sellers last year. So Oz knew this was going to be a jaw-dropping experience. She lay down, connected the new game to the microchip in her wrist and closed her eyes. A disembodied voice boomed from all directions in the darkness.

"Welcome to *Furiously Fast: Even Faster*. I am your virtual guide. *Furiously Fast* was a simple car-racing game that stimulated only one sense: sight. *Furiously Fast: Even Faster* is a multiplayer experience that stimulates all five senses. Not only can you see the cars, but you can touch them too. Feel the smooth leather of the seats, the cold metal of the exhaust pipe. You can hear the engines, smell the petrol, taste the competition in the air... Walk around, explore and, most importantly, win."

Oz opened her eyes and gazed around in disbelief, mouth gaping open. Cars zoomed past at unimaginable speeds and fans screamed from the sidelines as Oz found herself in the middle of a bustling racetrack.

"And remember, you will be unable to move your real body while playing the game. Any movements made will be made within the game only. To leave, say EXIT GAME aloud."

Oz ran at full speed to the start of the track to choose her vehicle, overtaking her friends Grit and Bearnice, who had logged into the same race. She'd done this a thousand times before, only this time it felt so real. She chose her favourite car (not the fastest option listed, but the lightest and most nimble). Colour and design options flashed in front of her eyes. She scrolled through them and settled on the hot pink flames. The disembodied voice was right – the smooth leather seats felt more real than anything Oz had ever touched before. Giddy with excitement, she slowly wheeled her car to the starting line, oblivious to the drama unfolding behind her.

"That's not fair!" Grit screamed in the distance. "I wanted that car. Why do you get to have that car? I hate this car. I hate you. I hate everything. EXIT GAME!"

Had Oz not been so distracted by her car's perfectly engineered steering wheel, she might have noticed the commotion that followed Grit's outburst. Had she not been so focused on the car's fourteen cup holders, she might have also noticed that Grit was still screaming.

"EXIT GAME!" he screamed again. "EXIT GAME! EXIT GAME! HEY GAME! I SAID EXIT! E-X-I-T! LET ME OUT!"

Much like a wildfire, panic spread quickly. Players everywhere were shouting "EXIT GAME!"... but nothing was happening. They were trapped. The commotion finally caught the attention of Oz and she made her way over to the chaos.

"Why are you all yelling?" asked Oz calmly.

"WE'RE TRAPPED! DOOMED! CONDEMNED TO GROW OLD IN THIS COUNTERFEIT WORLD!" howled Grit, banging his fists on the ground.

"What? Relax. You just have to force quit the game by heading to the data stream and entering the D7LP3 code. Duh," replied Oz.

"How did YOU know that?" asked Grit, mouth gaping open as he peered up at her from the ground.

"There's a lot you don't know about me," winked Oz as she climbed into her hot pink car and sped away, kicking up an extravagant amount of dust.

There were plenty of words you would use to describe Oz. Melodramatic was one. Smug was another. But her personal favourite was hero.

1 The adjective **retro** shows that *Furiously Fast* was an old-fashioned game.

Write down one other adjective in the second paragraph that shows this.

....

2 Which two other characters joined Oz on the same racetrack?

....

....

3 What car did Oz choose?

> The fastest and most nimble

> The lightest and most nimble

> The fastest and lightest

4 What two aspects of her new car distracted Oz from Grit's continued shouting?

....

....

5 Why do you think Oz said this line **calmly** while everyone else was panicking?

"Why are you all yelling?" asked Oz calmly.

....

....

....

6 Grit referred to the game as a **counterfeit world**. What do you think he meant by this?

....

....

7 Why do you think Grit emphasised the word **you** in this question?

"How did YOU know that?" asked Grit

....

....

....

....

8 Based on how she acted in the text, what two adjectives would you use to describe Oz? Explain your answer.

....

....

....

....

9 What makes this story fit the genre of science fiction?

....

....

....

Now it's your turn!

In this section, you will write the **introduction** to
a short **science fiction** story based on a writing prompt.

You may remember learning these aspects that can be included in stories:
an **opening**, a **build-up**, a **climax** and a **resolution**.

Your science fiction prompt is to write about
a scientist who has invented something world changing.

This could be anything from rocket boots to glow-in-the-dark
cauliflower to the world's first artificially intelligent toaster.

In this task, we're going to focus on writing an extended **opening**
(this is sometimes called an **introduction**).

If enough descriptive detail is used to introduce the setting, atmosphere
and characters (their appearance, personality, opinions and ambitions),
then the opening can be expanded across a series of paragraphs.

PARAGRAPH 1

This paragraph should introduce the setting.
Where was this invention designed? Was it in a clean,
high-tech laboratory or a filthy, makeshift garage?
What can be seen and heard?

PARAGRAPH 2

This paragraph should introduce the scientist.
Who is the scientist? What do they look like? What is their personality like?

PARAGRAPH 3

This paragraph should introduce the invention.
What is the invention? What does it look and sound like?
How and why might it change the world?

The first two sentences of Paragraph 1 have been written for you, but the rest is up to you! Here is some **vocabulary** that you might want to include in your story.

TIP!

The words with circular illustrations are nouns. Each noun is accompanied by three word pairs (words that frequently appear with it in stories).

amazing • enchanted • driverless
n.
flying car

young • billionaire • prolific
n.
inventor

advanced • amphibious • military
n.
hovercraft

human • evil • genetic
n.
clone

powerful • robotic • armoured
n.
exosuit

escaped • willing • unwitting
n.
test subject

human • broken • interplanetary
n.
teleporter

accidental • stranded • meddling
n.
time traveller

lifelike • military • advanced
n.
cyborg

rare • mistreated • telepathic
n.
mutant

evil • unfeeling • indestructible
n.
robot

flying • armed • annoying
n.
drone

gruelling

adj. difficult or draining;
like the effort of carrying
a huge bear

WORD PAIRS

gruelling **work**
gruelling **climb**
gruelling **schedule**

innovative

adj. creative or inventive;
like the genius who carved
the first wheel

WORD PAIRS

innovative **design**
innovative **idea**
innovative **technology**

astute

adj. clever or quick-witted;
like someone who understands
things quickly

WORD PAIRS

astute **reader**
astute **move**
astute **politician**

From the outside, you would never be able to tell that Apartment 14b had a top-secret laboratory hidden behind a fake bookshelf. The laboratory was cramped but well stocked with all the latest scientific equipment.

In this section, we'll be reading a script
based on part of the play *Macbeth*.

A script is a story that is written to be performed.
Scripts use **dialogue** and **stage directions**
and tell the performers how to say their lines.
The stage directions are in brackets.

First, we'll look at some vocabulary
that will help you understand the script.

Next, you're going to read
a brief summary of *Macbeth*.

Then, you're going to read the Mrs Wordsmith
version of a short scene from *Macbeth*.
Take your time and read it carefully.

4

Finally, use the text to help you answer the questions.
If you aren't sure about an answer, go back and read
the text again. All the information you need
is in the text.

tragedy

n. a play with an unhappy ending, especially for the main character

The play suddenly shifted from comedy to tragedy.

dialogue

n. what people in a book, play or film say out loud to each other

Their conversation was so witty it was almost like dialogue from a movie.

tantalising

adj. tempting but a bit out of reach

The tantalising apple dangled from the tree 20 metres above them.

prophecy

n. a prediction

The fortune teller's prophecies always came true.

hallucination

n. the sight, sound or feeling of something that is not actually there

After days without water, the explorer experienced a hallucination of a sparkling lake.

dagger

n. a short, sword-shaped knife

He knew he was in danger when he spotted the glint of a dagger under her coat.

Macbeth is a **tragedy** written by William Shakespeare in 1623. **Tragedies**, or tragic plays, are inspired by true events and have quite unhappy endings. Although *Macbeth* is based on real people and events, the tragedy is also full of the supernatural (like witches and ghosts).

Before we focus on one scene from the play, let's look at a summary of what has already happened in the story up to this point...

Macbeth is a military general who hears a **tantalising prophecy**. Three witches tell him that one day he will be the King of Scotland, but so will the children of his friend and fellow military general, Banquo.

Greedy for power and with support from his wife, Lady Macbeth, Macbeth secretly murders the current king, Duncan, and becomes the king in his place. But this isn't enough for the murderous couple. Knowing that Banquo's family is destined to be royalty makes Macbeth and his wife paranoid...

Although Macbeth immediately felt guilty for committing the first murder, he wants to protect his throne at all costs and can't stop thinking about the prophecy. To stop Banquo's family from stealing the throne, Macbeth secretly sends assassins to kill Banquo and his son. Banquo is killed, but his son manages to escape.

In the scene you are about to read, Macbeth is king. He is hosting a banquet for all his friends and allies, including Lennox and Ross, who don't yet know that Banquo is dead.

LADY MACBETH

(to Macbeth, who is anxiously walking around the room)

You're being a terrible host! A dinner party is supposed to be entertaining and fun.

The ghost of Banquo enters and sits in Macbeth's empty seat. Macbeth doesn't notice him yet.

MACBETH

Thanks for the reminder, my dear!

(raising his glass for a toast)

Over the lips and through the gums, look out stomach: here it comes. Cheers!

LENNOX

Won't you join us at the table, your Highness?

MACBETH
(ignoring Lennox's invitation)

The gang's all here, except for Banquo. I hope he's just being rude and that nothing terrible has happened to him...

ROSS

Extremely rude of him to miss this, I'd say. Your Highness, won't you join us?

MACBETH
(looking at the table and seeing no empty seat)

There's no room.

LENNOX
(pointing at the seat, which looks empty to everyone except Macbeth)

There's a place for you there.

MACBETH

Where?

LENNOX

(pointing at the seat again)

Right here. What's wrong, your Highness?

MACBETH

*(realising that it is Banquo's ghost sitting
in the seat that Lennox says is empty)*

Which one of you did this?

LORDS

(looking around but not seeing the ghost that Macbeth sees)

Did what?

MACBETH

(to the ghost)

I didn't kill you! Don't you shake your gruesome head at me!

ROSS

Everyone get up – the King is sick!

*The guests start to get up. Lady Macbeth looks nervously
at Macbeth then smiles politely at the guests and motions
for them to sit back down.*

LADY MACBETH

Sit back down, friends. This happens sometimes,
but he'll be alright – it's happened since he was a child.
He's just not feeling well. Don't pay him any attention
or it'll make him worse.

(pulling Macbeth aside and whispering urgently)

Pull yourself together!

MACBETH
(whispering to Lady Macbeth, his eyes wide)

I'm pretty together, considering the ghost of Banquo is sitting in my seat!

LADY MACBETH
(whispering back)

Cut it out! This is just one of those hallucinations you get when you're scared. Remember the floating dagger that led you to Duncan? These are just silly fantasies – shame on you! Now calm down – it's just an empty stool!

Macbeth takes a step toward the table, gesturing wildly, and Lady Macbeth tugs him gently back.

MACBETH

Can't you see it? Look!

(to the ghost)

So? Out with it! Can't you talk? Oh, who cares, anyway? If dead people are going to be climbing out of their graves, why should we even bother burying them?

The ghost exits. Macbeth and Lady Macbeth continue whispering together.

LADY MACBETH

Are you over it yet or what?

MACBETH

I know I saw him.

LADY MACBETH
(rolling her eyes)

Nonsense!

MACBETH
(shaking his head)

People have been killing each other since ancient times. But back then, when you murdered somebody, they stayed dead. Now, they come back to life and push us off our stools! This is too weird.

LADY MACBETH
(pointing to the waiting guests, who are sitting around the table looking confused)

You're ignoring your friends...

MACBETH

I forgot about them.

(to the guests, in a loud voice)

Don't worry. You know how I can be sometimes – weird, but nothing to worry about. Let's have a toast and I'll sit back down. Wine please!

The ghost enters again and Macbeth sees him.

MACBETH
(raising his glass for a toast, with a trembling hand)

Let's drink to everyone here, and to Banquo, who is most definitely, for sure, not here. Seriously, he's not here. Cheers!

LORDS
(raising their glasses)

Cheers!

1 Which guest appeared to be missing from the banquet?

....

2 How did Ross describe Banquo's behaviour?

a. hilarious ◯

b. strange ◯

c. rude ◯

d. unsurprising ◯

3 Why couldn't Macbeth sit down in the empty seat at the table?

....

....

4 What excuse did Lady Macbeth give for Macbeth's outbursts?

....

....

5 What did Lady Macbeth think the real reason was for Macbeth's outbursts?

a. He wasn't getting enough attention. ◯

b. His fear was making him hallucinate. ◯

c. He was being attacked by a ghost. ◯

d. He had caught the flu. ◯

6 **What did the ghost say to Macbeth?**

....

7 **Why didn't Macbeth tell everyone what he saw?**

....

....

8 **Why do you think the ghost appeared only to Macbeth?**

....

....

9 **Now it's your turn!**

Read the following story prompt and imagine how it might be acted out on a stage.

Prompt: Two sisters accidentally break their friend's cherished science fair trophy. Feeling panicked and guilty, the two sisters discuss what they should do about the accident.

Write a short script based on this prompt that actors could use to put on a play. Here are a few script-writing tips to help you get started:

1. Put the name of the person speaking followed by a colon on the left-hand side of the page. Write what you want them to say after the colon.

2. Put stage directions (telling the performers what to do or how to say their lines) in brackets on a separate line.

3. Try to show how a character is feeling through both their words and actions.

....

....

Poems can express a feeling, an idea or a story. Poems can be silly or serious, simple or complex, rhyming or not rhyming, follow lots of rules or follow no rules at all. Sometimes, poems use a range of writing devices.

Writing devices

Writing devices are techniques used to make poetry (or any writing style!) more interesting.

A **simile** compares one thing to something else (using the words **like** or **as**) in a way that makes it easier for a reader to imagine.

The bus raced past as fast as lightning.

A **metaphor** describes one thing as if it were another thing to help the reader imagine complex concepts easily.

The bus **was** a swirling typhoon.

Onomatopoeia is when a word sounds like what it means.

The bus raced past, **beeping** aggressively.

Personification is when an idea or thing is described in the same way you would describe a person.

The bus **laughed** and **jeered** as it raced past.

Hyperbole is when an idea is exaggerated for emphasis.

The bus raced past at a billion miles per hour.

In this section, we'll be looking at **four** styles of poetry,
all exploring the same short story:

Grit spotted his bus in the distance and began to sprint towards it.
He ran as fast as he could but missed it and had to walk home instead.
On his way, he found a snail heading in the same direction.
He stopped, picked it up and carried it with him.

Limerick

A limerick is a humorous poem consisting of five lines. The first, second and fifth have the same rhythm and rhyme. The third and fourth lines are typically shorter and rhyme with each other.

There once was a sad, sombre tale,
Of transport by bus, not by rail.
I ran straight outside,
But just missed my ride,
And was forced to walk home with a snail.

Haiku

A haiku is a three-line poem originally from Japan. The first line has five
syllables, the middle line has seven syllables and the last line has five syllables.

Take your time, slow down
Look around and you may find
An unlikely friend

Narrative

A narrative poem is a type of poem that tells a story.
It is often long and uses rhythm and rhyme.

Grit advanced at maximum speed,
Sweat dripping off his brow from persistence.
"I wish I'd left sooner," he thought to himself,
As he raced towards the bus in the distance.

He waved his arms like a frenzied conductor,
In the hope that the bus would wait.
But as it zoomed past and smoke filled the air,
He knew he was going to be late.

Feeling disheartened, discouraged, dismayed,
He let out a sigh and a groan.
The next bus wasn't for over an hour,
So he set out on foot to get home.

He walked along glumly, dragging his feet,
Leaving behind quite the trail.
When he noticed beside him, doing the same,
Was a small, insignificant snail.

The snail was heading in the same direction,
At a far slower pace through the sand.
So Grit showed kindness the bus had not,
"All aboard," he said, extending a hand.

Free verse

Free verse poems don't follow the rules.
They don't have to rhyme or use a structure like other poems.

A million mornings,
A million breathless sprints,
A million buses,
But I never seemed to catch one.

Run, run, run, run
Run, run, run.
Sweating. Sweating.

And I was still running, nearly there
But not quite,
As the bus chuffed out of sight,
Mocking me with each satisfied engine rev.

"Go home, slow poke!
No chance, snail-boy!
Maybe next time, snoozer!"

Hunched, slow,
Home-bound,
Angry,
I found a snail
And took it with me.

1 **These poems all use various writing devices. Copy out short examples of the following:**

a. Hyperbole in the free verse poem

....

b. Personification in the free verse poem

....

c. Onomatopoeia in the narrative poem

....

2 **The following is a simile from the narrative poem:**

He waved his arms like a frenzied conductor.

a. Why do you think Grit is being compared to a frenzied conductor?

....

....

b. Can you write a different simile to describe Grit waving his arms?

....

....

3 **Which two poetry styles have been written from the first-person perspective?**

....

4 **What do you think this line in the narrative poem means?**

So Grit showed kindness the bus had not

....

....

5 **The author uses repetition in the free verse poem to create a certain effect.**

What do you think is the effect of repeating the following words?

a. million: ....

....

b. run: ....

....

6 **Compare poetry styles.**

Draw lines to match the poetry style to the statement that best describes it.

Narrative	a poem that doesn't follow any rules
Haiku	a long poem that tells a story
Limerick	a three-line poem following a 5, 7, 5 syllable structure
Free verse	a humorous poem with five lines and a fixed rhyming structure

1

First, you're going to read the text of a **persuasive speech**.
The speech is given by Bogart, the fly, as he launches his campaign
to be elected as mayor. Take your time and read the text slowly.

2

Then, use the text to help you answer the questions.
If you aren't sure about an answer, go back and read the text again.

The purpose of a **persuasive speech** might be to persuade the audience of
a point of view or to inspire them to do something, like vote a certain way.

TECHNIQUES FOR PERSUASION

Emotive language and exaggeration

Using words with strong emotions behind them can persuade the reader. For example, saying something is **insufferable** is stronger than saying something is **unpleasant**.

Personal tone and direct address

Using words that make the reader feel directly involved (including **you** and **your** pronouns) can draw the reader in; for example, "Let me ask **you** something, **friend**".

Rhetorical questions

These are questions that make a point and do not require an answer. Asking questions can make the reader consider your point of view, for example, asking, "What is the point of that?".

Repetition

Repeating key points can help reinforce your ideas! Repeating key points can help reinforce your ideas!

TIP!

Certain types of repetition are especially effective. Often, people giving speeches will start the speech with an image or idea and then refer back to it at the end. This gives the speech a sense of completeness.

Bogart's campaign speech to become mayor of Alphabet City

Welcome, friends. As a fly myself, I am delighted to be here today at the convention for flies and maggots to talk to you about my upcoming campaign to become the mayor of Alphabet City. I am here to communicate one simple thing: vote smart and vote for Bogart. It is a pleasure to be amongst friends and I feel I speak for all of us when I say that this city has gone too far! Being as small as we are, the other inhabitants of Alphabet City think they can ignore us. Did you know that as many as 60% of the flies in this town have been swatted? That is just not acceptable. I am here to tell you that today is the day that everything changes. We, the true lovers of peace and quiet, have had enough of the constant chatter. We, the true lovers of all things gross, have had enough of these spotless streets. Let me tell you more about how I will make these changes.

Firstly, I vow to make this town quiet... silent, in fact. For too long, this town has been run by the let's-make-friends brigade, without even a second thought for the more antisocial members of our community. I ask you, do we really need to talk all the time? Every word that is spoken under Bogart's regime will require the speaker to show the correct paperwork. We want to know what people are saying, why they are saying it and when they are going to stop talking.

Secondly, fellow bugs, I intend to put an end to this insufferable reign of cleanliness and to reinstate an age of garbage everywhere. I believe in the right to be surrounded by trash and I will defend this right if it is the last thing I do. I don't care if the delicate amongst them can't stand the stench. I don't care if the Health and Sanitation Department finds it "criminally unhygienic and hazardous to public health". They had better get used to it because this is just the beginning of the rotten age of the filthy!

The other inhabitants of Alphabet City are too chatty, too cheerful and too clean. Luckily, however, it's not too late for the change we need. I may look puny, but rest assured, I am tough as an old leather boot and I will get things done. A vote for me is a vote well spent. Vote smart. Vote Bogart.

1 **What was the main purpose of this speech?**
Tick your answer.

a. to persuade the audience to be more polite   ◯

b. to explain how the rubbish is collected in Alphabet City   ◯

c. to organise a picnic   ◯

d. to persuade the audience to vote for Bogart   ◯

2 What did Bogart claim had happened to 60% of the flies in Alphabet City?

....

....

....

3 Circle two changes that Bogart said he would make if he were elected as mayor.

no more
chatter

more ice
cream for all

no more
picnics

garbage
everywhere

4 Find and copy out an example of **personal tone** in the first paragraph.

....

....

5 Find and copy out an example of a **rhetorical question** in the second paragraph.

....

....

6 Find and copy out two examples of **emotive language** in the third paragraph.

....

....

7 Can you find and copy something from the beginning of the speech that is **repeated** at the end?

....

....

8 Do you think that Bogart was persuasive in his speech? Explain your answer.

....

....

....

....

....

....

....

....

Now, it's your turn!

Meanwhile, at the convention for dogs and puppies, Grit is about to make his campaign speech to run for mayor too. Can you help him finish writing his speech? The introduction and first paragraph have been written for you.

Structure is very important when writing a persuasive speech.

Introduction

Start with an opening that **hooks** the audience into focusing on your speech. For example, you might open with a relevant surprising fact or engaging rhetorical question. Then, briefly outline all the main points you will cover in your speech.

Main section

A simple, clear structure is vital to getting your points across. Grit has three main points, so this section will have three short paragraphs. If Grit were to become mayor, he would make sure that:

Barking and growling become the official languages of Alphabet City

A game of fetch is played at least once per hour

Every resident of Alphabet City receives a delicious bone or a chew toy

Conclusion

Clearly signpost that your speech is coming to an end with a phrase like "**In conclusion...**" or "**My final message is...**" then briefly summarise your main points again. You may want to finish your speech emphatically with a memorable idea or rhetorical question.

Remember to include some of the following persuasive techniques in each paragraph:

Emotive language and exaggeration like **delectable bone** rather than **tasty bone**.

Rhetorical questions like **Who's a good boy?**

Direct address like **I know you love to play fetch!**

Repetition to reinforce your ideas!
Repetition to reinforce your ideas!

TIP!

Use connecting words (also known as connectives) throughout your speech. For example, first, second, third, next, before, earlier, finally, subsequently, then and to conclude.

The **introduction** and **first main body paragraph** have been written for you. It is your job to write the remaining **two main body paragraphs** and the **conclusion**:

The second main body paragraph should explore the idea "a game of fetch will be played at least once per hour".

The third main body paragraph should explore the idea "every resident of Alphabet City will receive a delicious bone or chew toy".

The conclusion should summarise your main points again.

Grit's campaign speech to become mayor of Alphabet City

57% of dogs have not yet played fetch today. That's over 200 dogs in Alphabet City who have been denied the joy of sprinting and catching a ball, stick or any other thrown object. I intend to fix that. Hello dogs, puppies, mutts, hounds and fellow canine creatures. I am here today to make three promises to you all if I am elected mayor. Barking and growling will be the official languages of Alphabet City. Fetch will occur citywide once an hour every hour. Everyone in this city will receive a delectable bone or chew toy.

Firstly, for too long we've had to keep our barks in. When was the last time you were able to bark freely? Too long ago! Under my rule, I will ensure that barking, growling, whining, howling, yipping and yapping are all official languages of this city. Or to put it simply... Bark! Bark! Bark! Bark!

REVIEW: TACO RESTAURANT

In this section, you will read a **critical review** of a restaurant. Critical reviews are commentaries on the characteristics and qualities of a work of art (like an exhibition, a book, a play or a film) or a place (like a restaurant or a hotel). They can be positive or negative and a person who writes one is called a **critic**.

The word "critic" comes from the Latin and Greek for "judge". Today, a critic gives their opinion in detail to help other people decide whether they want to spend money and time enjoying the artwork or place themselves.

First, you will read a review of a fancy restaurant, written by our favourite food-loving platypus, Plato.

Then, you will use the text to help you answer the questions. If you aren't sure about an answer, go back and read the review again. All of the information you need is in the text.

A critic at work

auspicious

adj. hopeful or encouraging

The rainbow on the day
of the race was an
auspicious sign.

forlorn

adj. sad and lonely

When I had to cancel my
birthday party and eat my
entire cake alone, I felt forlorn.

podium

n. a platform to stand on

The three best Olympic
gymnasts stood on the podium
to receive their medals.

ponder

v. to think deeply about something

Looking at the stars makes
me ponder the possibility of life
on other planets.

purveyor

**n. someone who sells
or provides something**

Bread Holes was the world's
largest purveyor of bagels
and doughnuts.

pretentious

**adj. trying to appear
grand or fancy**

I thought my friend was a bit
pretentious when she arrived at the
barbecue wearing a ballgown.

**More Like Taco Screams: Review of "Taco Dreams"
by Plato**

As I walked into the bright, clean space of Taco Dreams, I was overcome by the smell and sound of sizzling meat. It seemed like an auspicious start... until I realised that the sizzling sound was coming from the restaurant's sound system and the meat smell from its air vents. When I asked a waiter about this, he claimed that it was "the latest in sound and smell technology". Call me crazy, but I prefer a more natural experience.

Taco Dreams is the latest creation of star chef Nelly Nacho, pioneer of my favourite taco truck. Unfortunately, I think this time she's bitten off more than she can chew.

I soon discovered why they need to make the air smell so appetising here. It's because the actual portions are too small to smell like anything themselves. For a starter, I ordered the "Essence of Nacho", expecting a very big, very cheesy dish. What the waiter instead placed in front of me was just one dry tortilla chip, broken and stacked into three layers filled with a few cheese shavings, a scattering of chilli flakes and what would generously be called smudges of steak. They'll charge you extra for salsa.

With most of the starter stuck in the gap between my front teeth, it was on to the main event: the taco tasting menu, which was mouthwateringly described on their website as "a series of flavourful delights that will change your life forever".

The first taco consisted of thick strands of seaweed, woven into a circular shape and piled with caviar. This tasted like I'd been slapped in the face with a cold ocean wave, and not in a good way. The second was a single, forlorn black bean sitting on a tasteless disc of tortilla. A green drizzle hinted at guacamole that had seemingly run away to a tastier plate. But the grand finale, perched on a small podium as if the winner of a tiny food race, was a "reverse taco". This featured a small fold of tortilla bread, encased in a thin slice of meat... and all of the sadness in the universe.

Because (and only because) I was worried I might faint from hunger, I ordered the charmingly named "Mango Surprise" for dessert. As I watched the waiter carry a mango towards me, I almost wept with joy... but then I took a bite. It tasted like a parsnip. "Excuse me, but is this a parsnip?" I asked. The waiter gave me a sly smile as he said, "No, but we've engineered it to taste exactly like one." A tear slid down my cheek as I pondered who would do such a thing. I ordered a mango. I was expecting a mango. Why would I want something that tasted like a parsnip?

Tacos are one of the world's best inventions and Nelly Nacho is normally one of their most creative purveyors. But I ate no tacos at Taco Dreams, a pretentious nightmare that will haunt me, and my taste buds, for life.

1 **Whose restaurant was this?**

....

2 **Why did Plato have such high expectations for Taco Dreams?**

....

....

....

3 **Read this phrase from the text.**

... she's bitten off more than she can chew.

a. Why did Plato choose to write this?

....

....

....

....

b. **Bitten off more than you can chew** is an idiom. An idiom is a well-known expression that has both a literal and a figurative meaning. Circle the idiom that means **to reveal secrets**.

| to empty the cabinet | to spill the beans | to hop over the fence | to have a horse on your shoulder |

4 **A simile compares two things using the words like or as. Similes are used to help the reader imagine what is being described.**

Find and copy out two examples of similes in paragraph five.

....

....

....

....

5 **Using exaggeration in your writing is also called hyperbole; for example, saying it was hotter than the surface of the sun to describe a hot day.**

a. Find and copy out an example of hyperbole in the fifth paragraph.

....

....

....

b. Why do you think hyperbole was used in this review?

....

....

c. Can you rewrite the following sentence to include hyperbole?

I was very hungry.

....

....

6 **How did Plato feel about the food at Taco Dreams?**
Give two examples to support your answer.

....

....

....

....

7 **Reviews contain many adjectives and adverbs to help the reader imagine what the author experienced. This sentence from Plato's review isn't very engaging. Can you expand it into two sentences? Use descriptive language to show how the author is feeling whilst waiting for the dessert and to describe how the mango looks.**

I watched the waiter carry a mango towards me.

....

....

....

....

....

....

....

....

....

Now, it's your turn! Write a review of a fictional ice cream shop.

Structure your review in three paragraphs:

Introduction

Start with an opening that **hooks** the audience.
For example, you might jump straight into the action,
say something surprising, use an interesting quote
or ask a rhetorical question. The point is to make
your reader curious and excited to read on!

What was this ice cream shop called?
Why did you visit this ice cream shop?
What made this ice cream shop different
from all other ice cream shops?

Main section

This is where you can really get into the details of your
experience and use lots of descriptive vocabulary.

What did you order?
What did your order look and taste like?
How did eating it make you feel?

Conclusion

End your review with a short paragraph that summarises
the experience in just a few sentences.

Will you be coming back to this ice cream shop?
Would you recommend this ice cream shop?

Turn the page to find some vocabulary
that you might want to include in your review.

irresistible

adj. appealing and inviting; like something you can't help reaching for

WORD PAIRS

irresistible **temptation**
irresistible **colour**
irresistible **urge**

nauseating

adj. sickening or disgusting; like a rotten sandwich

WORD PAIRS

nauseating **stench**
nauseating **fear**
nauseating **sight**

savour

v. to enjoy or appreciate; when you eat very slowly so you can enjoy every bite

WORD PAIRS

savour **the taste**
savour **a mouthful**
savour **the moment**

In this section, we're going to focus on reading comprehension skills when reading non-fiction texts. Reading comprehension is all about reading a text carefully, taking your time and understanding it.

First, you're going to read an **explanatory text** about **how to spot disinformation online**. Take your time and read the article slowly.

Then, use the text to help you answer the questions.
If you aren't sure about an answer, go back and read the article again.
All the information you need is in the text.

---

vulnerable

adj. being easy
to influence or harm

clickbait

n. online content that is created
just to get people to click on it

troll

n. someone who pranks,
harasses or purposely confuses other
people online

bot

n. a computer program that
performs repetitive tasks and is
often designed to seem like a person

emotive

adj. resulting in a strong
emotional response

mislead

v. to purposefully cause
someone to get the wrong idea

manipulate

v. to influence or control someone,
usually for selfish reasons

fact-check

v. to investigate facts
and ensure that they are true

Disinformation Online

What is disinformation?

The term "disinformation" refers to false information that is shared with the intention to mislead people. It is dangerous because it is written with the intention to manipulate those who come across it in order to make them do something or act in a certain way. Disinformation is sometimes referred to as "fake news".

Fake news is nothing new, but thanks to new photo-editing technologies and the rise of social media, it has become an increasingly urgent issue. These freely available technologies make it very easy for anyone to make something up, make it look real and then spread it amongst huge numbers of people.

Disinformation affects us all, not just as individuals but as entire populations and societies. A particular concern for society as a whole is the sharing of false medical advice online. At best, this can result in people wasting their time and money on cures that do not work. At worst, people can seriously hurt themselves following dodgy advice. Another major concern is the sharing of distressing images and headlines that promote hateful and violent behaviours towards certain people or groups of people, both on and offline.

Where does disinformation come from?

It can come from anywhere. Online, anyone can say anything they want. In fact, anyone can claim to BE anything they want. This makes it difficult to decide if a person sharing information is really the expert they claim to be.

Disinformation is usually created by an individual or an organisation in order to achieve a particular goal. This could be something as simple as making money, but it could also be to promote a political party, to attack or humiliate a famous person or to share a specific point of view.

There are a few different ways that disinformation starts:

- An individual creates false information with the intention to mislead people.

- A bot is programmed to share false information across a number of platforms.

- A troll intentionally shares false information with the intention to harass or scare others.

DID YOU KNOW?

False information can also be spread online accidentally. Somebody may mishear or misunderstand certain facts, or be purposefully mislead. They might not realise that they are sharing false information with their friends and family.

How to spot disinformation

Here are some questions you can ask yourself to help you identify if something is true or false:

What is it saying?
Use your judgement to decide if the information sounds very surprising or suspicious. If it does, it could be false.

How does it make you feel?
Does this information make you feel especially angry, vulnerable or sad? If it does, it could be false, particularly if it refers to something shocking or unbelievable. The use of emotion grabs people's attention and drives them to take action. Although this can be used for good (like when you want to encourage people to donate to a legitimate charity), it can also be used to scare or anger someone into reading, spreading and remembering disinformation.

Does the topic in the article match the headline?
Sometimes, a "clickbait" headline gives a false impression
of reality in order to get people's attention. It can be tempting
to re-share articles without reading them, but if the content of
the article is different to the headline, it could be disinformation.

Conclusion

The purpose of reliable news sources is to prioritise facts over
opinions. Reliable news articles will not try to impose one particular
opinion or viewpoint on the reader. Always think before you share
articles that use emotive words like "evil", "terrifying", "shocking"
or "pathetic" in their headlines.

Fact-checking is one of the key ways for news outlets to ensure
that they do not spread disinformation. But not all news outlets
fact-check. You can check to see if the author of the article, or the
organisation as a whole, has signed up to a code of ethics (a set
of rules or guidelines) to help them produce responsible content.

It can be scary to think about lies spreading quickly on the internet,
but here's the good news about fake news: we can all fight it by
being more aware. In fact, most social media websites have a
button that allows you to report information that you think might
be fake, which means you can actively make a difference. By paying
attention and staying calm before sharing a wacky story, you can
help stop the spread of false information.

1 **Read the news headlines below.**

a. Which one do you think is most likely to be real?

Prime Minister admits plan to ban cheeseburgers in shocking confession

Could this band of rabid wolves be on its way to your city?

Water and energy shortages increase as heat waves hit India

Experts say 1 in 5 vaccines will melt your brain

b. Why do you think this is the least risky to share?

....

....

2 **What are two reasons that false information is easier to make and spread than ever before?**

....

....

....

....

....

....

....

3 Why does emotion help fuel
the sharing of misinformation?

....

....

4 What is the difference between a bot and a troll?

....

....

5 If you want to write a reliable news article,
how can you make it as reliable as it can be?
Tick all the correct answers.

a. Include very angry words in the headline.

b. Make sure to clearly separate facts from opinions.

c. Include links or references to external sources that support
the information.

d. Use an image that is stolen from a different website.

6 Now it's your turn!
Can you write a fake-news headline? Here are some examples to inspire you:

The sun is really just a big lamp!

Revealed: Parents' shocking plot to cancel school holidays

Could your socks be slowly killing you?

....

....

First, you're going to read an article about the Stonewall rebellion. Take your time and read the article slowly.

Then, use the text to help you answer the questions. If you aren't sure about an answer, go back and read the article again.

Content warning: This article includes references to violence.

VOCABULARY

LGBTQ+
an acronym standing for lesbian, gay, bisexual, transgender, queer (the plus symbol represents other sexual orientations and gender identities beyond these five)

lesbian
adj. attracted to people of the same gender (typically female)

gay
adj. attracted to people of the same gender

bisexual
adj. attracted to people of the same and different genders

transgender
adj. a person whose gender is not the same as their assigned sex at birth

queer
adj. not fitting traditional ideas of gender or sexuality

catalyst
n. an event or person that causes a change

riot
n. a group behaving in a violent and uncontrolled way

injustice
n. a situation that is not fair or not just

rebellion
n. a group behaving in a violent way in protest against an authority or government

marginalised
adj. treated as unimportant or insignificant and deprived of basic rights as a result

Wordsmith Weekly

Vol. 172   12 MAY   £3.00

STONEWALL: A REVOLUTIONARY TURNING POINT IN LGBTQ+ HISTORY

"African Americans can fight for their rights, Latinos can fight for their rights, women can fight for their rights, what about us?" – Mark Segal (2017), journalist and participant in the Stonewall rebellion

The events at New York City's Stonewall Inn on June 28th, 1969, were a major catalyst in the LGBTQ+ rights movement. Homosexuality was classified as a mental illness in America at the time, with many states denying basic human rights to those suspected of being part of the LGBTQ+ community. As a result, many LGBTQ+ people were forced to live their lives in secret.

In spite of this, New York City was home to a large, underground LGBTQ+ population and nightlife. This nightlife culture offered a space for LGBTQ+ individuals to feel free to openly socialise without fear of judgement. However, these spaces were far from safe. Police raids of gay bars were routine in the 1960s, with harassment, violence and arrests often taking place multiple times a week. The Stonewall Inn was one of these bars, but when a routine police raid began in the early hours of that June 28th, the events that unfolded are thought to have changed history.

It was the second time that week that the police had harassed the patrons of the Stonewall Inn, many of whom were of the most marginalised in the LGBTQ+ community (people of colour, transgender people and people without homes). These patrons resisted the police and violence quickly broke out. Amongst the protesters was Martha P. Johnson, a Black transgender woman who is often thought to have thrown the first brick, although she maintains that she only arrived at the scene after the events began. Within the LGBTQ+ community, people of colour and transgender people played a crucial role in this rebellion.

This uprising was classified as a riot at the time but is now known as the Stonewall rebellion – the important distinction being that a riot is a violent disruption of peace, whereas a rebellion is a violent disruption in protest against injustice from an authority or government. The actions of the patrons and onlookers at the Stonewall Inn were not a random act of violence but a protest against the inhumane treatment of their community.

News of the rebellion quickly spread, triggering a week of protests. Where previously the LGBTQ+ community lived in secret out of fear for their safety, the Stonewall rebellion inspired a demand for change. One month later, the first openly LGBTQ+ march took place in New York City. The protesters were demanding equality, but it was going to be a long road to achieving this goal. It wasn't until 2015 that same-sex marriage was legalised across all 50 states in America and the journey to achieving true equality and acceptance is still ongoing.

In some parts of the world, LGBTQ+ Pride Month falls in June every year in honour of the Stonewall rebellion, recognising how far LGBTQ+ rights have come and acknowledging the challenges that still exist. Pride is about acceptance and equality, but also about celebration. It offers people the freedom to celebrate themselves and be proud of who they are and whom they love.

1 When and where did the
Stonewall rebellion take place?

....

....

2 Why is the Stonewall rebellion considered
a catalyst in the LGBTQ+ rights movement?
Remember, a catalyst is an event or person that causes a change.

....

....

....

3 Why was New York nightlife culture so popular amongst
the LGBTQ+ community despite being unsafe?

....

....

....

4 On the night of the rebellion, how many times
that week had the police raided the Stonewall Inn?

....

....

....

5 Who is thought to have **thrown the
first brick** at the Stonewall rebellion?

....

6 Rebellion or riot?

a. Read through these fictional events.
    Draw lines to label these events based
    on the definitions of rebellion and riot.

A group of adults loot a
shopping centre in the hopes
of stealing electrical devices.

Rebellion

A group of women break
politicians' windows in the
hopes of earning the
right to vote.

Riot

A group of school children
destroy their cafeteria while
having a food fight.

b. Why do you think it's important to mark
    the distinction between a riot and a rebellion?

....

....

....

....

7 Can you name two marginalised groups that played a crucial role in this rebellion?

....

....

8 What do you think the word **ongoing** means in this phrase?

the journey to achieving true equality and acceptance is ongoing

....

....

9 What year was same-sex marriage legalised across all 50 states in America?

....

10 Why does Pride Month fall in June?

....

11 Why do you think Pride Month is so important to a lot of people in the LGBTQ+ community?

....

....

....

....

In this section, we're going to focus on reading comprehension skills when reading biographies and autobiographies. Reading comprehension is all about reading a text carefully, taking your time and understanding it.

A **biography** is the story of a person's life or experiences, written by somebody else.

An **autobiography** is the story of a person's life or experiences, written by the person themself.

First, you're going to read a short biography of the 19th-century nurse and businesswoman **Mary Seacole**. Take your time and read the article slowly.

Then, you're going to read a short extract from Seacole's autobiography, **The Wonderful Adventures of Mrs. Seacole in Many Lands**. This was written a long time ago in old-fashioned English, so you may need to read it a few times to get a sense of the meaning. Don't worry if you don't understand every sentence!

Use both texts to help you answer the questions. If you aren't sure about an answer, go back and read the texts again. All the information you need is in there.

Before you get started,
let's look at some helpful vocabulary.

racism

n. the act of treating someone differently because of their race, ethnicity, nationality or colour

There is no place for racism in today's world.

prejudice

n. judgements made about someone without using facts or actual experience

Education helps people see beyond their own prejudice.

dwell

v. to stay or linger on something

Let's look forward and not dwell for too long on the past!

recollections

n. memories

My recollections of that holiday are a little blurry, but I'm fairly sure there was a roller coaster ride.

yearn

v. to long for or want something very badly

On dark winter days, I yearn for the sun.

scarcely

adv. hardly or barely at all

There is scarcely one person here whose birthday you haven't forgotten!

A Biography of Mary Seacole

Who Was Mary Seacole?

Mary Seacole was born in 1805, in Kingston, Jamaica. Seacole was born a "free person" at a time when many black people in Jamaica were enslaved. Her father was Scottish and her mother was Jamaican.

Seacole was exceptionally brave and lived an extraordinary life, breaking social barriers to do things that other 19th-century women could only dream of. She travelled far and wide, deepening her knowledge of medicine wherever she went and helping people, even in the face of racism and prejudice.

Early Life and Education

Seacole's mother was a healer and ran the Blundell Hall lodging house where many sick or injured soldiers would stay. It was watching her mother treat patients at Blundell Hall that first sparked Seacole's own interest in medicine. By the young age of 12, Seacole was helping her mother run the business and was picking up skills in traditional Jamaican and African healing and medicine.

Travels

Seacole travelled to England twice as a teenager. She also travelled around the Caribbean to Cuba, Haiti, Panama and the Bahamas. She even went as far as Crimea, in eastern Europe.

Crimean War

In the early 1850s, when Seacole heard about the soldiers going off to fight in brutal battles in the Crimean war, she was determined to go and work as a nurse in the war effort there. She applied to the British War Office, requesting to be an official army nurse, but they turned her down. Seacole didn't let that stop her. She raised the necessary funds and organised her own journey.

Upon arrival in Crimea, Seacole set up the British Hotel as a place where soldiers could go to rest and be treated. The British Hotel was very close to where the fighting was happening and Seacole was known to go to the front line to care for wounded soldiers, even while the fighting was taking place. Seacole returned to England after the war and published her autobiography in 1857. It became a bestseller.

Extract from **The Wonderful Adventures of Mrs. Seacole in Many Lands**

by Mary Seacole

a house offering beds and food to paying guests

an old fashioned word for a female doctor

It is not my intention to dwell at any length upon

the recollections of my childhood. My mother kept

a boarding house in Kingston, and was, like very

many of the Creole women, an admirable doctress;

in high repute with the officers of both services, and

their wives, who were from time to time stationed at

good reputation

DID YOU KNOW?

"Creole" is a word with a complex and rich history. At the time when Seacole was writing her autobiography, it referred to people of mixed European and African descent who spoke a language called Creole, particularly those born in the West Indies.

Kingston. It was very natural that I should inherit her tastes; and so I had from early youth a yearning for medical knowledge and practice which has never deserted me. When I was a very young child I was taken by an old lady, who brought me up in her household among her own grandchildren, and who could scarcely have shown me more kindness had I been one of them; indeed, I was so spoiled by my kind patroness that, but for being frequently with my mother, I might very likely have grown up idle and useless. But I saw so much of her, and of her patients, that the ambition to become a doctress early took firm root in my mind; and I was very young when I began to make use of the little knowledge I had acquired from watching my mother,

upon a great sufferer – my doll.

supporter

Lazy

1 **Write an A next to the sentence that describes autobiography and a B next to the sentence that describes biography.**

a. This kind of text is often written many years after the person has died.

b. This kind of text gives us a direct insight into the person's thoughts.

2 **Here are some sentences from the texts that were not included in the extracts above.**
Read them and write an **A** if you think they are from the autobiography or a **B** if you think they are from the biography.

a. So I made long and unwearied application at the War Office, in blissful ignorance of the labour and time I was throwing away.

b. Seacole's husband fell ill soon after they were married and she looked after him.

c. The night was made a ruddy lurid day with the glare of the blazing town; while every now and then came reports which shook the earth to its centre.

3 **Tick all the countries referenced in the biography that Seacole travelled to.**

England   Argentina   Cuba

Panama   Australia   Haiti

4 What year was Seacole's autobiography published?

....

5 Using the biography, can you find and write down an example of a time when Seacole showed bravery?

....

....

6 How did the British War Office react to Seacole's application to become a nurse?

....

....

7 What topic is Seacole writing about in the extract from her autobiography?

| her time in Crimea | her early life | her grandmother |

8 How did Seacole practise her nursing skills as a child?

| She practised on a doll. | She practised on a pet lizard. | She practised on her mother. |

9 **Tick the quote from Seacole's biography that tells us something similar to the following quote from her autobiography.**

In this quote, Seacole is talking about her mother.

"It was very natural that I should inherit her tastes; and so I had from early youth a yearning for medical knowledge."

Seacole's mother was a healer and ran the Blundell Hall lodging house where many sick or injured soldiers would stay.

Her father was Scottish and her mother was Jamaican.

It was watching her mother treat patients at Blundell Hall that first sparked Seacole's own interest in medicine.

10 **An autobiography gives the reader clues about the writer's personality.**

Can you draw a line from these phrases to the corresponding personality traits?

who could scarcely have shown me more kindness had I been one of them

curious

the ambition to become a doctress early took firm root in my mind

determined

I had from early youth a yearning for medical knowledge

appreciative

Now that you've written your own stories,
you're more than ready to edit someone else's!

1 Read through this text and correct the errors.

All the errors in this text have been underlined and it's your job to fix them using skills that you learned in the rest of this book. The underlined mistakes include spelling, punctuation and grammar errors.

For decades, Bearnice campaigned

to make water fighting an official

Olympic sport. She wrote letters,

signd petitions and even held protest

marches – all in an attempt to

perswade the Olympic committee

to take the sport more seriously. She firmly beleived that water fighting

was not just for tenth birthday party's and hot summer afternoons, but

that it was meant to be competed in at a national scale in arenas

across the globe. And, after years of asking the Olympic committee

finally said yes.

The first round of Olympic water fighting was a total disaster.

Newspapers worldwide referred to it as a "national embarassment".

Nobody was familiar with the rules so the players imediately desended into utter chaos. They kicked screamed set traps and even fought with non-regulation liquids like olive oil.

"Who's terrible idea was this?" cried members of the audience.

"This was an awful decision" sighed members of the Olympic committee.

Bearnice knew what she had to do. So she set to work and writes up all the water fighting rules in an official rule book. She published her first (and only!) draught the day before the second round of water fighting. Surely nothing could go wrong now.

However, the mischeivous players had other ideas. They found hundreds of ways to get around Bearnices rules. The rules said no kicking so they elbowed each other instead. The rules said no olive oil so they used mayonnaise. The fight was, once again, utter chaos.

Maybe I should try and write a second draught..."

Bearnice muttered sheepishly.

2 Can you improve this story?

You've edited to make corrections. Now, let's try editing to improve a text. Here is a section of the story that wasn't included in the text above.

"Team A hid behind the fallen tree. Team B ran forwards. Team C refilled their weapons with water."

These three sentences describe a moment of action in the first Olympic water fight, but there is hardly any detail in the description.

Can you rewrite these sentences as a paragraph? Feel free to be as creative as you like and expand your ideas across multiple sentences. Don't forget to use adjectives (words that describe nouns) and adverbs (words that describe verbs) to make your sentences more exciting.

So far in this chapter, we have done a lot of reading practice, but really the best reading practice is reading for fun!

One of the best tips for reading is to shop around! Ask your friends and family what they read for fun. You might be a huge fan of spy stories, or books about rare species of scorpions, and not even know it yet.

To inspire you, here's a sneak peek into the Mrs Wordsmith book club group chat. **A book club** is a group who meet to discuss a book they've all read. Our characters are debating what to read next...

BOOK SQUAD CHAT: Stay true to your shelf
Oz, Bearnice, Shang High, Bogart, Grit, Yin, Yang, Armie, Brick, Plato

Oz
I couldn't put down **Trowbridge Road** by Marcella Pixley.

I gobbled it up in a week.

What are we reading next???

Bogart
YOU'LL NEVER STOP ME!!!

Oz
Relevant comments only please.

Shang High
What is real? What is everything made of? What can we ever truly know?

Oz
I said relevant comments only please.

Shang High
Those are relevant!

What's the point of existence?

Let's try to find out by reading **Philosophy** by DK

It'll blow your mind!!!

Bearnice
That sounds really insightful, Shang High

But please please please please
can we read **Feminism Is...** by DK next?

It's insightful and illustrated and insightful

And asks important questions about
gender and the world

AND it's insightful

Grit
I think you forgot to mention how
insightful it is, Bearnice

Yin
It's illustrated?

If you want illustrations, then we should
read **Turtle in Paradise**!

It's a graphic novel by Jennifer L. Holm
and Savanna Ganucheau

It's full of family secrets and pirate treasure

Grit
YAWN

Yin
Pirate treasure isn't boring, Grit

What's your suggestion then?

Grit
Dinosaur by David Lambert, DUH!

It's got everything you could ever want

Dinosaurs

and digging up BONES!

Oz
If you don't take this seriously, Grit,
I'm going to join a different book club.

Armie
Or how about Ebony Joy Wilkins' biography
of **Katherine Johnson**? She was a NASA
mathematician and it was her calculations
that helped us land on the moon!

Shang High
Amazing! Maybe it'll help me answer
the question...

Do aliens exist?

Bearnice
Sounds very insightful, Armie! I'm in!

Oz
Perfect!

Yin
Count me in!

Grit
Okay sure... but is it about bones?

Oz left the chat

This book club clearly needs your help! What was the last thing you loved reading? Write your answer in the group chat.

You have been added to the chat

Bogart
OBEY ME!

Grit
Ignore him

Bearnice
Sorry about Bogart

What do you think we should read next?

Yin
Yeah, help us out!

Draw
yourself
here

You

···

···

Pages 10–11

1 **a.** proper: Grit
   common: poem
   b. proper: Oz
   common: sculpture
   c. proper: Brick, Thailand
   d. proper: Armie, Tuesdays
   common: lessons
   e. proper: Plato
   common: restaurant
   f. common: factory

2 **a.** abstract: generosity
   concrete: teacher
   b. concrete: trousers
   c. abstract: freedom
   concrete: shed
   d. concrete: firefighter, cats, houses
   e. abstract: chaos
   concrete: bedroom

3 concrete nouns: pineapple, nail, lemon
   abstract nouns: peace, danger, love

Pages 12–13

1 **a.** V **b.** N **c.** N **d.** V **e.** V **f.** N **g.** N

2 **Your answers might be something like:**
   a. Yin and Yang made a promise that they would replace the vase.
   b. Shang High made Armie promise to help him fix his saxophone.

Pages 14–15

1 **a.** subject: Bogart
   object: Brick
   b. subject: Grit
   object: tail
   c. subject: Bearnice
   object: film
   d. subject: ghost
   object: mansion
   e. subject: Armie
   object: vault
   f. subject: Shang High
   object: guitar

2 **a.** V **b.** S **c.** V
   d. O **e.** O **f.** V

3 **Your answers might be something like:**
   a. Shang High **b.** rubbish **c.** Armie
   d. the stew **e.** her phone **f.** a scarf

Page 17

1 **present tense:** "Grit watches TV every day." and "Armie wakes up at 6am."
   past tense: "Oz slept through the whole movie." and "Bearnice accidentally tied her shoelaces together."

2 **a.** Yang loved spinach.
   b. Bearnice always forgot her pencils.

Pages 18–19

1 **a.** are **b.** is **c.** are **d.** am

2 **a.** was **b.** were **c.** were **d.** was

3 **present progressive:** "Oz is singing in front of the mirror.", "Yang is firing arrows from behind the trees.", "Bearnice is hiding the note inside a locket." and "Plato is drinking maple syrup straight from the bottle."
   past progressive: "Bogart was sending anonymous hate mail.", "Shang High was wearing a helmet." and "Armie was hacking into the company's database."

4 **Your answer might be something like:**
   I was eating my dinner.

Pages 20–21

1 **a.** PP **b.** PP **c.** PS **d.** PP **e.** PS

2 **a.** had started **b.** had judged
   c. had photographed
   d. had turned **e.** had waited

3 **Your answers might be something like:**
   a. Bearnice has destroyed the cake.
   b. Armie has bought a car.

Pages 22–23

1 **a.** The table was destroyed by Yang.
   b. All the burgers were eaten by Plato.

c. The brand new sports car was driven by Oz.

d. The red bike was ridden by Armie.

2 a. A   **b.** P   **c.** A   **d.** P

Pages 24–25

1 a. Armie   **b.** Shang High   **c.** Plato

2 Your answers might be something like:

a. I will travel the world when I'm older.

b. The ex-footballer must learn a new sport this year.

c. They may move to a new country someday.

d. She ought to learn how to drive.

e. He might become a famous singer.

Pages 26–27

1 a. Yin loves **this** waterpark.

b. Plato ate **his** waffles in **a few** seconds.

c. Bearnice eats apples **every** day.

d. Bogart plans to use **these** tools to take over **the** city.

e. Shang High lost **those** gloves last night.

f. Oz has **many** hobbies.

2 a. this, an   **b.** Our   **c.** Those
d. your   **e.** Many   **f.** my   **g.** more

Pages 28–29

1 a. They   **b.** hers   **c.** ours   **d.** them
e. She   **f.** theirs   **g.** It   **h.** They

Pages 30–31

1 The concert tickets, **which** Bearnice got for her birthday, were from Brick.

Shang High, **whose** neck is incredibly long, always hits his head on door frames.

Yin, **who** looks just like Yang, is often blamed for her sister's troublemaking.

2 a. where   **b.** whose   **c.** which
d. that   **e.** which

Pages 32–33

1 a. Oz fainted **when** she forgot her lines on stage.

b. **After** a long week, Bearnice relaxed at a spa.

c. Grit chased his tail **until** he finally caught it.

d. **After** spending all day collecting ingredients, Plato was excited to start cooking.

e. **When** the lights went off, everyone started screaming.

f. Brick ate two lunches **even though** he wasn't that hungry.

g. Bogart covered his ears **whenever** Bearnice started to sing.

h. **After** crossing the crumbling bridge, Yin and Yang breathed a sigh of relief.

i. **Whenever** he was lost for words, Shang High felt like his tongue was tied in a knot.

Pages 34–35

1 a. Shang High, who had just put his headphones on, was feeling peaceful.

b. Plato wrote out his grandfather's pancake recipe, which had been handed down over four generations.

c. Yin angrily chased Yang, who had just purposefully smashed her science fair trophy.

d. The theme park, which had been open for 40 years, was closing down.

2 Your answers might be something like:

a. was extremely hungry

b. was covered in heavy books

c. had been a birthday present

d. he knew he could easily dodge

Page 36

1 a. wondering **b.** Laughing   **c.** stopping

Page 37

1 a. Even though there was a "DANGER" sign on the door, Brick crept into the abandoned hotel.

  b. Plotting his next prank, Bogart sat in his underground lair.

2 Your answers might be something like:

  a. , who had just slipped on a banana peel.

  b. After his friends threw a loud party that kept him awake,

  c. , listening nervously for approaching footsteps.

Pages 38–39

1 a. Oz demanded that the shop give her a refund.

  b. Plato recommends that you sample his latest recipe.

  c. Shang High requests that you listen to his album.

  d. If I were an environmental scientist, I would clean up the oceans.

2 Your answers might be something like:

  a. If I were to be elected as mayor, I would change this city for the better.

  b. I recommend that you vote for me if you want the amount of litter to decrease.

  c. I request that you give me a chance to show you how wonderful this community could be.

  d. It's not enough to just demand that we change things for the better.

Pages 42–43

1 a. Q   **b.** C   **c.** C   **d.** Q   **e.** E

2 Your answers might be something like:

  a. Is Oz very selfish sometimes? **or** Oz is very selfish sometimes, isn't she?

  b. Are oranges orange? **or** Oranges are orange, aren't they?

  c. Can't pigs fly? **or** Pigs can't fly, can they?

Pages 44–47

1 a. Shang High's **b.** children's

  c. ducks'   **d.** Lucas'   **e.** Plato's

  f. people's   **g.** Dickens' **h.** Bogart's

2 a. Brick's archnemesis won the 100m race.

  b. The children's teacher surprised them with a silent disco.

  c. The pineapple trees were planted by the mayor's husband.

  d. They all agreed that the bakery's bread was the best bread.

  e. James' suit came from the tailors.

  f. Oz and Bogart's cunning plan was starting to work.

  g. Bearnice couldn't believe her eyes when she saw Yang's pose.

3 Your answers might be something like:

  a. Grit's doughnuts are all gone.

  b. The sun's heat was oppressive.

  c. Because of the chilli, Plato's tongue was on fire.

  d. The clouds' game was terrifying.

Pages 48–51

1 a. Bearnice declared, "This is the worst day of my life."

  b. "I can't believe you won!" cried Brick.

  c. "It's not fair," moaned Plato.

  d. Oz commanded, "Everyone look at me!"

  e. "What should I do next?" pondered Armie.

2 a. "Don't," snapped Oz, "touch my phone."

  b. "Imagine," gasped Shang High, "a three-week music festival."

  c. "How much," questioned Grit, "is that dinosaur bone?"

d. "I can't," admitted Plato, "eat anymore."

e. "I shall," cackled Bogart, "tie everyone's shoelaces together."

f. "I buried the treasure," confessed Yang, "in the back garden."

g. "I think," confessed Brick, "I might have been working out too much."

Page 52

1 **T**he expedition... middle of **w**inter, **B**earnice... (**n**ot realising... in the **A**rctic)... Arctic **f**oxes...

Page 53

1 a. The Arctic fox, known for its white fur, is able to camouflage itself well in the snow.

b. *Chiroptera*, meaning hand wing, is the scientific name for bats.

c. Bearnice ate the last, and coincidentally biggest, slice of cake.

2 a. Yin, known for her excellent behaviour, was the teacher's favourite.

b. The artwork, painted by Vincent van Gogh, was stolen.

Page 54

1 a. Oz travelled to Paris (the capital of France).

b. Grit (the grump!) disliked everyone.

2 The attic (which Armie told me never to enter) is full of gadgets.

Page 55

1 a. Oz – who was in love with herself – gazed at her reflection in the mirror.

b. Just then, Grit – Plato's friend – walked into the room.

c. Bearnice – known for her hugs – squeezed Bogart way too hard.

2 a. Grit – after hours of digging – found a dinosaur bone.

b. A sweet smell – perhaps of cookies or cakes – wafted from the kitchen.

c. Shang High – after four hours of listening – paused the music to sneeze.

Pages 56–57

1 a. unfinished thought: "I'm not going to..." mumbled Plato.

suspense or tension: Slowly, they crawled into the dark cave...

word or words have been removed: Blue whales... migrate to middle and low altitudes in the winter.

2 Your answer might be something like:
He'd done it!

He was convinced that someone, or something, was following him...

Page 58

1 a. A record amount of snow fell that afternoon: it was eight metres deep by 4pm.

b. Plato loves to bake all kinds of treats: cakes, pastries and tarts.

c. Shang High is a talented musician: he writes all of his own songs.

d. Oz waltzed down the catwalk: she had never felt more confident.

e. Grit only ever wanted to be in three places: his bed, his armchair or his garden.

Page 59

1 a. Yang forgot to lock the back door; Yin hated it when she did that.

b. Oz took a selfie in the garden; Bearnice tried to get to know all the flowers.

c. To make a pie, Plato needs flour, butter and salt for the pastry; plums, apples and sugar for the filling; and cherries to decorate.

d. The sailor has been at sea for four months; he writes home to his family every two weeks.

e. Armie built a time machine that could also bake brownies; it was his greatest invention yet.

Pages 62–63

1 a. trans **b.** bi **c.** tri **d.** semi

2 Your answers might be something like:

a. biceps: Bogart flexed his impressive biceps.

b. triathlon: Shang High started the triathlon in the lead.

c. translucent: The jellyfish were translucent.

3 triangle, semiformal, biweekly, transform

Pages 64–65

1 a. tele **b.** photo **c.** micro **d.** aero

2 a. televised **b.** microsecond
c. photosynthesis **d.** photocopying
e. aerospace

Pages 66–67

1 a. the study of the Earth's surface
b. a system of government in which people vote for their political representation
c. to calm down or bring peace to
d. They're afraid of heights.

2 a. against **b.** money
c. believe **d.** first

Pages 68–71

1 a. threw **b.** piece **c.** too
d. pair **e.** know **f.** guest

2 a. aisle, isle **b.** wait, weight
c. draft, draught **d.** serial, cereal

e. write, right **f.** descent, dissent

3 a. device **b.** devise **c.** devise
d. device **e.** devise

4 a. Whose **b.** Who's **c.** whose
d. Who's **e.** whose

Pages 72–75

1 hate–loathe
huge–enormous
beautiful–scenic
sleepy–fatigued

2 a. wicked **b.** innovative **c.** vivid

3 lively > boisterous
best > finest
endless > unlimited
a brave > an intrepid
a cunning > a devious
a thoughtful > a pensive
a knowledgeable > a wise
smiled > grinned

4 spotless–filthy
strong–frail
messy–neat
spicy–bland

5 Your answers might be something like:

a. smug
b. lavish
c. disappointed
d. heartfelt
e. energetic
f. public
g. superior

Pages 76–77

1 small: tiny (synonym), microscopic (stronger synonym)
big: huge (synonym), colossal (stronger synonym)
happy: content (synonym), overjoyed (stronger synonym)
sad: miserable (synonym), inconsolable (stronger synonym)

beautiful: attractive (synonym), stunning (stronger synonym)
love: adore (synonym), idolise (stronger synonym)

2 **a.** Brick   **b.** Paris   **c.** Bogart
  d. Oz   **e.** Plato

Pages 78–79

1 **a.** stubborn, determined
  b. speechless, tongue-tied
  c. cunning, astute

Page 82

1 **a.** fictitious   **b.** contentious

2 **a.** spacious   **b.** cautious

Page 83

1 **a.** residential   **b.** beneficial
  c. official

2 **Your answers might be something like:**
  a. glacial: Armie shivered in the glacial winds.
  b. confidential: Bearnice accidentally revealed the confidential information.

Pages 84–85

1 **a.** incredible   **b.** possible
  c. laughable   **d.** considerable
  e. comfortable   **f.** noticeable
  g. responsible   **h.** visible

2 **-able:** agreeable
  -ible: responsible
  -ably: miserably
  -ibly: visibly

3 incredible, responsible, miserably, considerable, visibly, possible, noticeable

Pages 86–87

1 **-ant:** vacant, assistant, dominant, significant, radiant, brilliant
  -ent: repellent, independent, argument, president, present, resident

2 **a.** vacant   **b.** dominant
  c. president   **d.** independent
  e. significant

3 **a.** assistant   **b.** argument   **c.** present

4 resident, brilliant, president, repellent

Pages 88–89

1 **a.** attendance   **b.** tolerance
  c. diligence   **d.** prominence
  e. residence   **f.** evidence

2 **a.** vacancy   **b.** decency

3 residence, evidence, tolerance, decency, diligence, attendance, prominence

Pages 90–91

1 **a.** receive   **b.** achieve   **c.** piece
  d. relief   **e.** deceived   **f.** retrieve
  g. conceited

2 receipts, inconceivable, thieves, chief

Pages 92–93

2 **a.** awkward   **b.** immediately
  c. desperate   **d.** embarrass
  e. interrupt

3 **a.** stomach   **b.** foreign
  c. mischievous   **d.** persuade
  e. determined

Pages 96–105

1 **Your answer might be something like:**
"Tigers are large, strong and fierce" **or** "Tigers are at the top of the food chain."

2 **Your answer might be something like:**
"You can tell the other animals do not respect Anansi because they **"barely cast him a second glance"** and refer to him as **"a spider"** rather than by name."

3 **Your answer might be something like:**
"Anansi said it to flatter (or compliment) Tiger so she would be more likely to help him."

4 Your answer might be something like: "Being confident or bold in a way that is shocking or rude"

5 a. "Anansi would rather we didn't focus too much on that afternoon."

b. Your answer might be something like: "To draw the reader in and make them feel part of the story"

6 Your answer might be something like: "Anansi had been trying capturing techniques that he wasn't very good at."

7 Your answer might be something like: "Anansi wanted to make Snake think that lots of animals were talking badly about her so she would want to prove them all wrong."

8 Your answer might be something like: "The author was showing the reader that Anansi was pretending to be helpful in order to trick Snake."

9 Your answer might be something like: "Snake is proud and self-obsessed so she wanted everyone to think that she is very long."

10 Your answer might be something like: "All the jungle animals were desperate to see Snake captured with their own eyes. Mouse scurried underground, Hippo swam swiftly along the river, and Orangutan swung hurriedly through the trees. When they arrived, they stared in astonished silence."

Pages 106–117

1 Outdated

2 Grit and Bearnice

3 The lightest and most nimble

4 The steering wheel and the cup holders

5 Your answer might be something like: "Oz remained calm because she knew how to exit the game."

6 Your answer might be something like: "A world that looks exactly like the real one but is still fake"

7 Your answer might be something like: "Grit emphasised **you** because no one knew that Oz was an expert player of *Furiously Fast*."

8 Your answers might be something like: "**Surprising** because she has lots of hidden interests and talents" **or** "**Confident** because she knew how to exit the game and didn't panic like everyone else"

9 Your answer might be something like: "The story involves advanced technology, like the microchip in Oz's wrist or a virtual reality game that feels like the real world."

Pages 118–127

1 Banquo

2 c

3 The ghost of Banquo was sitting there.

4 Macbeth was not feeling well.

5 b

6 The ghost said nothing.

7 Your answer might be something like: "None of the dinner party guests knew that Banquo was dead." **or** "Macbeth didn't want anyone to know that he ordered for Banquo to be murdered." **or** "Macbeth didn't want his guests to know that he was seeing something they couldn't see."

8 Your answer might be something like:
"The ghost only appeared to Macbeth because he ordered Banquo's murder." **or** "The ghost only appeared to Macbeth because he felt guilty for killing Banquo."

Pages 128–133

1 a. "A million mornings" **or** "a million breathless sprints" **or** "a million buses"
   b. "Mocking me with each satisfied engine rev"
   c. "zoomed"

2 Your answers might be something like:
   a. "Conductors wave their arms around when leading an orchestra. Similarly, Grit was waving his arms in a wild and uncontrolled way when trying to get the bus to wait."
   b. "He waved his arms like an Olympic gymnast."

3 Limerick and free verse

4 Your answer might be something like:
"Grit is stopping to help something slower than himself even though the bus did not stop for him."

5 Your answers might be something like:
   a. "It makes it seem like missing the bus happens all the time, creating the sense that the character's struggle is never ending."
   b. "It gives the impression that the character is running very far and putting in a lot of effort."

6 Narrative: a long poem that tells a story

Haiku: a three-line poem following...

Limerick: a humorous poem with five lines...

Free verse: a poem that doesn't follow any rules

Pages 134–141

1 d

2 60% of the flies have been swatted.

3 no more chatter, garbage everywhere

4 Your answer might be something like:
"I'm here to tell you that today is the day that everything changes."

5 Your answer might be something like:
"I ask you, do we really need to talk all the time?"

6 Your answer might be something like:
"insufferable reign of cleanliness" **or** "rotten age of the filthy"

7 Vote smart. Vote Bogart.

8 Your answer might be something like:
"Yes, Bogart was persuasive because he used a range of persuasive techniques, including rhetorical questions and repetition."

Pages 142–151

1 Nelly Nacho

2 The restaurant was run by the pioneer of his favourite taco truck.

3 a. Your answer might be something like: "To communicate that Nelly Nacho has taken on more than she can handle in a way that is funny (because it's food related)."
   b. to spill the beans

4 "This tasted like I'd been slapped in the face with a cold ocean wave" **and** "perched on a small podium as if the winner of a tiny food race"

5 a. "and all the sadness of the universe"

b. Your answer might be something like: "Hyperbole is used for dramatic effect to entertain the reader."

c. Your answer might be something like: "I was so hungry that I could have eaten a dinosaur!" **or** "I had never been more hungry in my entire life."

6 Your answer might be something like: "Plato did not like the food at Taco Dreams. He complained throughout the review and referred to the food as "too small" and a "pretentious nightmare"."

7 Your answer might be something like: "I watched hungrily as the waiter approached my table. He was carrying a ripe, juicy mango."

Pages 152–157

1 a. Water and energy shortages increase as heat waves hit India

b. Your answer might be something like: "The information in the others is quite shocking and difficult to believe and some of them use very emotional language."

2 New photo-editing technologies and the rise of social media make it easier to make and spread disinformation.

3 The use of emotion grabs people's attention and drives them to take action.

4 A bot is a computer program designed to seem like a real person, whereas a troll is a real person who purposefully harasses or confuses others online.

5 b, c

6 Your answer might be something like: "Panic! All the fish have vanished!"

Pages 158–163

1 New York City's Stonewall Inn on June 28th, 1969

2 The Stonewall rebellion inspired a demand for change and a month later the first openly LGBTQ+ march took place in New York City.

3 The nightlife culture was a space for LGBTQ+ people to socialise without fear of judgement.

4 Twice

5 Martha P. Johnson

6 a. Rebellion: "A group of women break…"
Riot: "A group of adults loot a…" and "A group of school children…"

b. Your answer might be something like: "While both involve groups behaving violently, it is important to remember a rebellion is a protest against an injustice."

7 People of colour and transgender people

8 Your answer might be something like: "Still happening" **or** "Still in progress"

9 2015

10 June is the anniversary of the Stonewall rebellion.

11 Your answer might be something like: "Pride is a way for LGBTQ+ people to celebrate themselves and be proud of who they are and whom they love."

Pages 164–171

1 a. B   **b.** A

2 a. A   **b.** B   **c.** A

3 England, Cuba, Panama, Haiti

4 1857

5 Your answer might be something like:
"She wanted to work as a nurse in the Crimean war."

6 Your answer might be something like:
"The British War Office rejected Seacole."

7 her early life

8 She practised on a doll.

9 It was watching her mother treat patients at Blundell Hall that first sparked Seacole's own interest in medicine.

10 curious: "I had from early youth a yearning…"

determined: "the ambition to become a doctress…"

appreciative: "who could scarcely have shown me…"

Pages 172–175

1 signd > signed
perswade > persuade
beleived > believed
party's > parties
asking the > asking, the
embarassment > embarrassment
imediately > immediately
desended > descended
kicked screamed set traps > kicked, screamed, set traps
Who's > Whose
decision" > decision,"
writes > wrote
draught > draft
mischeivous > mischievous
Bearnices > Bearnice's
Maybe > "Maybe
draught > draft

COOKED UP BY MRS WORDSMITH'S CREATIVE TEAM

Creative Director
Craig Kellman

Pedagogy
Rochelle McClymont
Eleni Savva

Academic Advisor
Emma Madden

Lead Designer
James Sales

Designer
James Webb

Writers
Tatiana Barnes
Amelia Mehra
Jill Russo

Artists
Brett Coulson
Giovanni D'Alessandro
Holly Jones
Phil Mamuyac
Aghnia Mardiyah
Nicolò Mereu
Daniel J. Permutt
Maggie Ziolkowska

No animals were harmed in the making of these illustrations.

Project Managers
Senior Editor Helen Murray
Senior Designer Anna Formanek
Project Editor Lisa Stock

Senior Production Editor Jennifer Murray
Senior Production Controller Mary Slater
Publishing Director Mark Searle

First published in Great Britain in 2022 by
Dorling Kindersley Limited
A Penguin Random House Company
DK, One Embassy Gardens, 8 Viaduct Gardens,
London SW11 7BW

The authorised representative in the EEA is
Dorling Kindersley Verlag GmbH. Arnulfstr. 124,
80636 Munich, Germany.

10 9 8 7 6 5 4 3
003-328329-Dec/2022

A CIP catalogue record for this book
is available from the British Library.
ISBN 978-0-24155-470-8

Printed and bound in Malaysia

For the curious
www.dk.com

mrswordsmith.com

MIX
Paper | Supporting
responsible forestry
FSC™ C018179

This book was made with Forest
Stewardship Council ™ certified
paper - one small step in DK's
commitment to a sustainable future.
For more information go to
www.dk.com/our-green-pledge

The building blocks of reading

READ TO LEARN

LEARN TO READ

| Phonemic Awareness | Phonics | Fluency | Vocabulary | Reading Comprehension |

READICULOUS

Readiculous App
App Store & Google Play

Word Tag App
App Store & Google Play

OUR JOB IS TO INCREASE YOUR CHILD'S READING AGE

This book adheres to the science of reading. Our research-backed learning helps children progress through phonemic awareness, phonics, fluency, vocabulary and reading comprehension.